In Transition

cx

IN TRANSITION

Navigating Life's Major Changes

W. WAYNE PRICE

MOREHOUSE PUBLISHING
Harrisburg, Pennsylvania

Copyright © 2002 by W. Wayne Price

Morehouse Publishing
P.O. Box 1321
Harrisburg, PA 17105

Morehouse Publishing is a division of The Morehouse Group.

Design: Corey Kent
Cover art: Window of Beehive Church, Great Skellig Island, Ireland
           Corbis/Michael St. Maur Sheil

Library of Congress Cataloging-in-Publication Data

Price, W. Wayne, 1938–
    In transition : navigating life's major changes / by W. Wayne Price
        p. cm.
    ISBN 0-8192-1904-5 (alk. paper)
        1. Life change events—Religious aspects—Episcopal Church.
I. Title.
BV4908.5 .P76 2002
248.8'6—dc21

                                                    2001044526

Printed in the United States of America

02 03 04 05 06   6 5 4 3 2 1

For Jo Anna,
who gracefully shares the entire journey

❧

Contents

Introduction

Each night when I go to sleep, I die; and the next morning when I wake up, I am reborn.
—*Gandhi*

A blacksmith's hammer of crisis forges the mature identity of nearly every person. The heat of the bellows and the blows of the steel hurt us; they often seem relentless, endless. On the other side of painful change, loss, failure, or other personal disasters, however, we may become better people than we ever thought possible. Yet who in a sound state of mind would ever have wished for the pain? Comments from those who, like Job's comforters, tell us that everything works out for the best cut like knives into soft places the hammer could not touch. Nevertheless, suffering, the ability to embrace it, and the capacity to rise above its causes define each of us, more or less.

In most suffering, "why" questions are answered either in the continuing ring of the hammer or by deafening silence. Somewhere in the pain or on the slope away from it, we inevitably ask ourselves, "Where to from here, and how do I get there?"

During more than forty years in my role as an ordained minister, I have stood by and cried with hundreds of people who, at that one time or time and again, endured more than they ever believed possible, sometimes more than I thought they could endure. Many lives are changed forever when tragedy strikes. Consider the family members whose lives took a dramatic turn when their young son/brother died in a war. I stayed with them day after day, sharing a tiny piece of their distress. Imagine how the death of a child who drowned affected an extended family forever. When they tell me about the child, the event seems as immediate as yesterday. I listened to a woman nearly beaten to death by the man who said he loved her. She could not decide which was worse, her shoulder-shaking sobs or her bruised and bloody face. Many of us could cite similar examples of painful times. Those whose pain I have known bore different names, but their pain was no less than that of Shakespeare's tragic characters—Othello, Lear, and Ophelia—and part of the lot of "Everyman." I cannot recall, even as a very young pastor, ever telling them that it would be all right; I never knew their breaking points or the intensity of their losses. Mostly I just sat and cried with them.

Just as we struggle with the rearrangement of life in the midst of and after a tragedy, we wrestle as well with the consequences of the changes we want and pursue. Parents want their children to go to college, but their absence from home leaves a great emptiness. We want those new jobs in exciting new places, but we have trouble leaving behind the life we have made. We want to retire and do many things we had little time to do when we were working, but we find it difficult to live without office, title, and authority. Even changes in our lives that are envied by others are often accompanied by the loss of other good things. Loss hurts.

The question this book attempts to answer is: Can a particular loss—from wherever the hammer blows come—ever contribute to making someone's life all right, to making a person better than before, to bringing him or her to a greater sense of God's love? What part has God in all this, at its beginning, middle, or end? Who would dare suggest God as a source of the storm? Who, indeed, at such a time would dare say with the Apostle Paul, "Rejoice in the LORD always" (Philippians 4:4)? Yet after the trial by fire comes an inevitable opportunity for refashioning the self. The heat that hardens the clay also melts the wax; each of us continues to become, emerge, and change. I have seen it happen. I know it to have happened repeatedly—in my own time in the fire, on the anvil, along that long and rocky road of transition.

I have come to an uneasy acceptance of suffering as part of our natural existence; some suffering seems completely willy-nilly and some the result of bad human choices, but none of it is the result of God's intention. Suffering must be lived through, but it is best lived through with some hint of hope in the process. I have come just as surely to a sense of the presence of God when I sit alongside those in pain as when I share their joy. I have also sensed the presence of God during my own times of difficult transition.

Name a major life transition of any sort: I can probably remember people who faced it, although each faced it in his or her own unique way. Of two persons experiencing the same kind of change, I can recount how one was left embittered and the other came through with a greater depth of spirit. How can that be, especially when both professed similar faith and both enjoyed almost equally the privileges of cultured background, high intelligence, and extensive support? In part, their differing reactions lie in their intentions, the foundations of their faith, and whether that faith was dynamic or static. That the answer also lies partially hidden in mystery I know to be true, not only out of my professional experience and as a practical theologian, but also from the time I have spent on my own rugged pathway.

I have lived long enough to experience and observe many of the "thousand natural shocks the flesh is heir to"; I know best those sorrows in which I nearly lost my belief in my own future and saw no value in the present. Three times, I have been brought not only to my knees, but also to a place of utter prostration. I suffered failure and loss in the three functional areas of my life that I held and still hold most dear—academics, family, and profession. Each situation was more difficult to handle than the one before.

The first of these came during a period of my life when I was overextended. I served as minister of a suburban church, taught English at a university, and took graduate courses in English. Toward the end of my course work, with language examinations behind me and a good grade-point average, I took on a larger parish on a full-time basis. My wife also became pregnant with our first child. At the same time the graduate faculty changed its testing methodology. I failed the qualifying examinations. I had never failed anything in my life and became terribly distraught.

Later, in the mid-eighties, my family suffered through a poorly managed period during our daughters' adolescences. One daughter underwent serious emotional struggles; before she recovered, the other daughter developed problems as well. I recounted these bleak years in a book called *Confessions of a Perfect Parent*.

My third transitional crisis occurred as the result of an intransigent church conflict, the end of a forty-year Baptist ministry, and a severe depression. More of that story will emerge in the pages to follow. Suffice it to say here that most transitions tend to be somewhat predictable and that every transition has embedded in it some seeds for new life. I have learned, grown, and deepened because of all three of these life crises.

My profile might fit a vast segment of our culture. I grew up hard, as a parentified child with too many adult responsibilities. I was rewarded with admiration and privilege for my role as a good boy. I was a perfectionist with a need to be competent. A caregiver, ambitious to the point of being driven. Successful. The hammer seems to fall harder on such people; true to form, it drove me into the ground. No addictions, criminality, or immorality. Perhaps my failures resulted from unrealistic expectations, unanticipated changes, and just plain circumstances, but my pain proved to be as sure and as severe as anyone can imagine—relentless and lasting, each time for double-digit months. Perhaps my doctor was right: "You made yourself sick." I did and I know it now.

Am I the recipient of more hurts than others? Hardly. Such is the human condition. I know many people whose lot has been far more difficult than my own. I have greatly admired many whose courage, faith, and resilience have easily outstripped my own. So, what makes this confessional exercise worthwhile? Simply this: After three sessions of hammering, I have discovered a pattern as well as some resources that have been incredibly and gracefully healing, instructive, and formative— even at my age.

At the end of 1997, I concluded my ministry to a church I had served for nearly seventeen years. The church was engaged in a protracted and intransigent conflict. Although I did not realize it at the time, I also concluded a Baptist ministry of forty years. On January 1, 1998, for the first time in my adult life, I looked at an almost blank future—no profession, no career, no job, with little soundness of mind and a broken heart. For many weeks, I sat at a table, worked jigsaw puzzles, and cried. However, what I still possessed far outweighed what I had lost, although at the time I hardly realized it.

I think now about Jacob's dream of the ladder stretching from heaven to earth, angels of God ascending and descending upon it. At daybreak he says, "Surely the LORD is in this place and I did not know it" (Genesis 28:16b). Had he been told as much in the dream, he could not have heard or seen the truth: the truth had to become his own discovery, his own realization.

I had known for many weeks what I would do about resigning from my position. I was in no condition to make any plans beyond December 31, 1997. I retained sufficient wit and memory, however, to know that I had not handled my prior family crisis very well a decade earlier or my academic crisis some twenty years before that. I was beginning to realize I was a slow learner. In June, I had placed myself in the care of a fine physician who provided both medication for depression and incisive talk therapy. Instead of withdrawing or shutting myself off from others, I accepted the wisdom and support of my family and many friends. These supportive people helped me move from the jigsaw puzzles into meditation and reflection.

During the final days of 1997, I determined that if I was to heal and recover from my fourteen-month ordeal and find my place in the wisdom of God, I must adopt a plan of action in addition to medication and counseling. I discovered—instead of action—a plan of inaction. Not passivity, but inaction. As I moved my books and office to my home, I remembered the spiritual autobiography of the late William Barclay of the University of Edinburgh, Scotland. His nanny often said at day's end, "Come, Willie. Let us put our things away and see where we stand." I was putting my things away in order to see where I stood. Piles of book boxes filled the garage. Boxes of pictures and mementos from my church office sat along the walls of one room in our home, the room that would become my new office. The clutter in the house proved to be a pathetic reflection of my inner life. For one so goal-oriented, so action-centered, the thought of having no specific goals threatened my sense of identity.

In those bleak days of January, after most of the tears had stopped and as medication and therapy continued, I began to come to grips with exhaustion, depletion, a sense of loss, anger, and all sorts of irrational fears. I also began to appreciate what I still had. Cards, letters, flowers, phone calls, and promises of prayers came from people from around the country. More local friends than I could ever have expected regularly embraced me, physically and emotionally. My wife stood steadfast and courageous for me, although she herself boiled with anger. Through their many telephone calls and visits, our daughters and sons-in-law proved themselves loyal and loving. My physicians were beacons of compassion, but tough and demanding. I worked hard at physical exercise, recalling my late teacher and mentor Carlyle Marney, who often said, "Work is to depression what worship is to exhaustion."

As I searched for a way through the angst, I conferred carefully with several wise and trusted friends, determined to do better than I had done in previous crises. I continued to meet with a men's support group, as I had for twenty-five years. I tried to do very little else except listen.

The psalmist kept speaking to me.

Be still before the LORD, and wait patiently for him;
do not fret over those who prosper in their way,
over those who carry out evil devices.
Refrain from anger, and forsake wrath.
Do not fret—it leads only to evil. (Psalm 37:7–8)

A Wonderful Discovery

As I grasped for something to hang onto, I remembered the order of the monastic day. It reminded me of the need to let go of much that troubled me, so that I could rest and find true peace. Although my former faith tradition knows little of monastic life or of the ancient Daily Office, I had been a sometime student of liturgical disciplines, particularly of the Trappists, whose monastery I had once visited, and whose best known monk—Thomas Merton—I had met. I had purchased a copy of the Episcopal *Book of Common Prayer* in 1963, but had paid little attention to the Daily Office—the services for daily prayer.

The Daily Office, while not referred to by that title, existed in Judaism and was continued by the early church. It served as a daily clock, calling for prayers at each juncture of the day. The Book of Daniel refers to the hours of prayer. The Acts of the Apostles refers to the disciples going up to the Temple at various hours in observance of the custom. Later, in monasteries, the full complement of prayer times set the rhythm of each day. My adopted tradition, the Episcopal Church, includes Morning Prayer, Noonday Prayer, Evening Prayer, and the office of Compline in its Prayer Book. The word "compline" itself comes from the same root as "complete," or tying up the loose ends of the day. It was the Compline office of the day—the last hour of the Daily Office before retiring to sleep—to which I was drawn.

My plan began to unfold like a gift from God. I devoted lengthy periods to disciplines involved in letting go of whatever encumbrances I could release. My prayers involved surrendering to my situation. I realized in time that I had already begun the process of letting go, as much out of depression, hopelessness, and desperation as from a positive discipline. After my prayers, I turned to the discipline of waiting. One of my old bibles bears the marks from an assortment of pens I used to underline various themes in my close readings of the Psalter; one of those themes was waiting.

I was free enough of financial constraints that I had one entire year to work with, more if I needed additional time. I chose to devote the first six months to the process of letting go. I had much that needed to be released, including issues from much earlier in my life. I planned to use the final six months of 1998 as a period of waiting. These were not rigid time structures; each included some overlap or anticipation of the other. Such a plan would have been nearly impossible if I had been employed. My situation happened to be ideal for the process of healing because I could give myself completely to letting go and waiting. I never took that luxury for granted.

I had some ideas about what I needed to let go, but I could not have anticipated either the process or the outcome. Neither could I have entered the waiting period with a clear sense of what would fill the void left as I turned loose more and more. Even now, well on the other side of the year, I am not certain about my future. I am certain only that God will accompany me in the journey and will be there at my end. I offer my ongoing experience as both testimony and recommendation.

I continue to struggle with loss, grief, anger, pain, change, and self-doubt. Wounds heal slowly, and the scars remain sensitive and visible. I am sometimes surprised by unexpected reminders of those events that changed my life forever and by how many of the emotions I experienced then continue to haunt me. After the long year of spiritual discipline, therapy, medication, and encouragement from family and other people of faith, I am looking ahead more than backward. Surely the Lord is in this place, but now I know it.

CHAPTER ONE

Letting Go

❧

Evensong and Compline are not an intentional part of the Baptist tradition in which I grew up and ministered. However, Sunday evening "preaching services," Wednesday night prayer meetings, evening bible readings, and prayers for various occasions certainly offered me some of the same end-of-day time with God as the ancient Daily Office has always done for untold thousands. Sometime in late elementary school, two evening hymns became a part of my bed-time preparations: "Now the Day Is Over" and "The Day Thou Gavest Lord Has Ended." I often sang them silently to myself before sleep.

> Now the day is over, night is drawing nigh,
> shadows of the evening steal across the sky.

> The day thou gavest, Lord, is ended,
> the darkness falls at thy behest;
> to thee our morning hymns ascended,
> thy praise shall sanctify our rest.

As I grew older, I learned to treasure evening hymns, these and many others. They follow a pattern very similar to Compline: praise to God for the gift of the day; a request for forgiveness of sins and/or protection from the power of evil even in the night; a restful, peaceful sleep; and an awakening/resurrection at the dawn. I learned early in life that sleep and rest were a form and symbol of letting go, of trusting oneself to God in the darkness and sleep.

For centuries, Christians everywhere and monastics in particular have done what I had done as a child, but in a much more orderly, intentional, and thorough manner: with more scripture, prayers, and canticles. Just before retirement for the day, the brief service of Compline serves as a kind of "funeral" for the day just ended, a letting go, a turning loose. The content, however, is not mournful, although it always includes confession of sin, recognition of the difficulties of life, and even awareness of evil. Those aware of and touched by difficult transitions, sin, trouble, and evil, are upheld by the merciful hands of God, the divine Parent unto whom holy men and women commend themselves in the sure hope of waking to the light—the resurrection at the next dawn.

This is the pattern. The leader begins, "The LORD Almighty grant us a peaceful night and a perfect end." There follows a prayer of confession, an assurance of pardon, and the Gloria. One or more psalms about the evening and sleep may be read (Psalms 4, 31, 91, and 134). A brief lesson is read: Hebrews 13:20–21 or 1 Peter 5:8b–9a; then an evening hymn is sung. Versicles and responses follow—"Into your hands, O LORD, I commend my spirit." Next, a "LORD, have mercy" and the Lord's Prayer.

A series of short prayers are said and the service concludes with the Song of Simeon ("Nunc Dimittis")—

"LORD, you now have set your servant free to go in peace as you have promised . . ." The service concludes with a blessing.

During the period of my own transition, that service from the Daily Office sounded a waiting but previously silent chord in my heart. I saw in it the need we all have to end each day by letting go of our sins—those of omission and commission—our errors, failures, grievances, resentments, grudges, and burdens. I moved gradually from emphasizing the current day and began to recognize that I needed to let go of much that had accumulated over a lifetime. I could see that in times of crisis we all need a longer period of Compline in which to let go of what has built up to gigantic proportions, has taken a long time to develop, and has occupied us for months—in some cases, years. The period of six months I allowed myself to do the work of letting go may not have been enough. I had much to release—good-byes not handled well, my own sense of failure, my many losses, a great deal of hurt and anger, and a damaged sense of who I was and who I am.

Perhaps the most significant and difficult release proved to be my perfectionism. I thought I had done well with that one when I wrote the book about parenting. I had always believed that if I worked very hard and lived morally and with spiritual integrity, I could avoid the traumas that others fell into. My daughters taught me that being an imperfect parent did not mean that I was a bad parent. My friends have been teaching me that simply because my tenure in a church ended in disaster, my good ministry there has not been nullified. My therapist has enabled me to work harder on letting go of my perfectionistic expectations that allow any falling-short to damage my sense of self-worth. In reality, then, Compline became for me not simply a brief service at the end of each day, but a six-month service of worship on a single theme. I studied the hymns, the psalms, and the biblical narratives that included the themes of letting go, release, and self-emptying. I was constantly conscious of or in a struggle with what I needed to let go, especially those issues, attitudes, and methods of functioning that seemed most difficult to release from my life. I discovered bit by bit that letting go involves both danger and risk. I risked losing what and who I was without much idea about who and what I would become. I gradually realized that the daily discipline of letting go had to become more than a small part of a six-month discipline—or of a year-long practice. For me, letting go has become a lifetime commitment to self-examination, release, and hope. Whatever one develops, builds up, becomes, and holds onto cannot be faced, confessed, and released in a single, general service of prayer. But every long journey begins with a single step.

My bible study gave me a different perspective, more personal than ever before. A new and existential reading of the Exodus story proved to be one pivotal revelation, perhaps even a parable of my personal circumstances, as it has been for individuals, groups, and races of people for thousands of years. The Exodus suggests a release from everything negative, evil, debilitating, and even idolatrous. Out of bondage, free in the wilderness, and facing opportunity on the other side of the Jordan River, the Israelites became fearful and anxious. Change always seems to elicit anxiety. Water was scarce, the food unfamiliar and not regularly available, and the leadership proved to be an easy target. "If only we had died by the hand of the LORD in the land of Egypt, when we sat by the fleshpots and ate our fill of bread" (Exodus 16:3). As difficult as slavery had been, the Israelites had not let go of their past. The devil they had known seemed better than the devil they did not know. The behavior of the Israelites reminds me of a comment one of my teachers, Carlyle Marney, was fond of repeating: "The way most of us hang onto our sins, we would conclude that they were the best things that ever happened to us."

I had and have my own share of "weight and the sin that clings so closely" (Hebrews 12:1). My entire life has been directed toward goals, achievement, and success. I set very high standards for myself and for others—higher standards than some wanted for themselves. Of course, perfectionism itself is a form of idolatry at its worst; at the least, it is a guarantee of personal failure. Such was my bondage, my Egypt, my Red Sea.

During those early weeks of my crisis, I lived in the desert between Egypt and a promised land I could not imagine. Those arid places were my personal wilderness. I could not move forward until I had made progress in letting go. In the past I had advised many people who sought my pastoral care to do the same thing, but one's wisdom seems always more applicable to others than to one's self.

At the extreme other end of letting go—this time in a very positive way—is the story of Jesus coming to earth and finally going to the cross; he let go of a great deal. Saint Paul, thinking about the cross much later, said that Jesus "emptied himself" of divine likeness, took upon himself the form of a human slave, and became obedient to death on the cross (Philippians 2). No other "letting go" can match the Incarnation. No other letting go better illustrates the way we can bring about new life for ourselves and for others than sacrificial suffering and even death.

The psalms also echo the theme of letting go:

Into your hand I commit my spirit;
you have redeemed me, O LORD, faithful God.
(Psalm 31:5)

Repeatedly the psalmists give up their own defenses, let go of their own securities—sometimes false securities—in order to take refuge in God and to allow God to protect them.

You who live in the shelter of the Most High,
who abide in the shadow of the Almighty,
will say to the LORD, "My refuge and my fortress;
my God, in whom I trust." (Psalm 91:1–2)

The psalmists also seek release from their sins. The best known and loved of these psalms is Psalm 51.

Wash me thoroughly from my iniquity,
and cleanse me from my sin. (Psalm 51:2)

One recalls almost automatically all manner of biblical stories in which people let go of family and native land, like Abraham, who responded to God's call to move his family and possessions to an unidentified location that would be revealed on the way (Genesis 12:1–3). In several other biblical stories, people were called upon to give up their livelihoods; for example, the disciples who left their fishing nets to follow Jesus. Saint Paul even left his family and religious community after his conversion to Christianity. The disciples, Saint Paul, and a host of early evangelists—even early martyrs such as Stephen and James, who followed Jesus in the ultimate act of letting go—all serve as illustrations of sacrifice. They willingly gave up their former ways of living and some gave up their very lives.

As they speak to us in our own crises, biblical stories and characters suggest that as long as life moves along steadily and with little upheaval, we assume a posture of well-being. Temporary freedom from diseases of the body, demons of the mind, sins of the soul, fractures in relationships, failures in our work—in other words, the absence of any known catastrophe around the next bend in the road—lures us into a sense of well-being that may be more fragile than we know. However, crisis looms ahead somewhere in all our lives; given proper attention, it uncovers our bondages, idols, excess baggage, and destructive memories. The "sin that clings so closely" tends to become our master sooner rather than later.

Perhaps for many of the psalmists, total letting go and trusting God came when their personal circumstances left them few other choices. I suspect as much in my own situation. These times may be few and rare; nevertheless, they are real and eventually are a part of the experience of every human being.

Letting Go of Our Former Roles

Loss of a role or position inevitably will be a burden for all of us at one period of life or another. Retirement, divorce, a move to a new community, the end of the parenting years, loss of stature in the community, loss of work or professional position—these often prove to be difficult because they are losses of roles that once defined us.

Loss of Role and Status

A competent and well respected mayor died rather suddenly. His widow received a great deal of support in her grief. Family, neighbors, friends, community leaders, and church members rallied around her. Unfortunately, as the months turned into years, she became increasingly angry, far beyond the kind of transitional anger most people experience with the loss of a loved one. Anger could be understood as a normal part of the loss of her mate; in her case, severe anger developed from the loss of her role as wife of the mayor of her town. Her anger pushed people away from her and she became somewhat isolated and lonely, although she continued to involve herself in community activities. She could not see and was not willing to recognize that she was no longer the wife of the mayor, no longer a celebrity at banquet tables, no longer meeting dignitaries who were greeted by the mayor. She could not let go of the title, "First Lady."

I can relate to the issue of loss of a role. One day I was senior minister of a downtown church in a prestigious community, well known and respected in the area and in the larger life of my denomination; the next day I woke up without employment, title, or portfolio. For several months I struggled with the issue of my identity apart from the work I had loved for forty years.

An early adolescent question surfaces, "Who am I?" Sadly, and most unfortunately, who we are is often tied to what we do or to the status we have achieved. We should cringe to hear a parent say, "She's the smart one in the family," or "He's our athlete." Most of us can recall elementary school days as if they were yesterday, as well as the identity of each classmate. One fit the role of "brain," another "teacher's pet," another the class clown, another a dancer or musician. Later in life, we take our identity from the work we do. Meet someone at a party, in church, in travel and the first question is: "What do you do?" Our careers often identify us, along with education, income, house size and neighborhood, automobile make and associations. The loss of any or all of them leads us to the conclusion that we are no longer anybody, or at least we are not who we thought we were.

Loss of the Parenting Role

Consider the often-repeated story of the parent who cannot let go of a son or daughter. The first jolt comes when the daughter goes off to college, but she still comes back home occasionally. In reality, most college students do not return for more than short-term visits. They may come back to work for the summer; they may come home to live for a year sometime during the transition from student to worker; they may keep their rooms and many belongings in their parents' homes for a long time. In actuality, however, they have begun to move steadily toward independence and some renegotiation with their parents about an adult-to-adult relationship.

As an aside, I am not unaware of the families in which parents half-jokingly say, "I haven't had a problem with letting my son/daughter go; he/she keeps moving back home!" These young people themselves see risk and change as a threat and tend to hold on to the security of house and family.

The parents, however, tend to be the ones who have the most difficulty letting go of their children. No one should be surprised. The growing-up tasks take the young person's entire lifetime, and they are usually ready to move out and onto the next stage of their experience. Parents, on the other hand, experience the loss of a role—including clearly defined tasks in relation to their children and certain connections with community institutions—signaling their need to redefine who they are. How does one let go of what has been so all consuming? The process takes time as well as a measure of courage.

In the words of that text to which I keep returning, all of us are called to let go of "every weight and the sin that clings so closely, and . . . run with perseverance the race that is set before us" (Hebrews 12:1). Part of that journey, that race, that pilgrimage includes leaving behind some position, status, role, or function—either because it no longer serves us or because our role no longer exists.

Loss of Identity as a Spouse

The role of husband or wife may cease to exist, either for a time or for the balance of one's life. How difficult it is to let go of a relationship that has in many ways defined us; yet divorce demands we do just that. The weight of a "former" marriage creates enormous burdens, but the loss of role and that part of one's identity may be the heaviest. To be husband, wife, mother, father provides a title, status, role, and one aspect of identity. Divorce ends part of that structure and identity. Even if the termination was done with some grace, not being who we have been as married persons requires restructuring, even reinventing ourselves. A new life cannot be adequately fashioned and structured until the divorced person is able to let go of both the former spouse and of his or her previous role as husband or wife.

The death of a spouse also forces many to cross a bridge of transition, alone and empty. The house seems deafening in its silence. Simple maintenance previously shared by the couple falls on a single pair of shoulders: yard work, car repairs, housekeeping, even a task as simple as changing a lightbulb seems like an enormous burden. Evenings enjoyed together, shopping, day trips, and community projects no longer have any appeal. I have often in my grief work with parishioners suggested that the loss of a spouse may be the most profound loss anyone can sustain. Nothing will ever be the same. But I am also quick to suggest that life can indeed be good again for those willing to construct a new way of being.

For those who travel the narrow and rocky path mandated by divorce or death of a spouse, dealing with social structures may be the most difficult. The newly single person may not be welcome or comfortable in the couples' bridge groups or dinner parties. Customary social invitations may become fewer. Close friends may distance themselves. Not only must such persons let go of the spouse they lost; they may need to let go of some friends, activities, and even dreams that once held such importance for them.

Loss of Occupation Identity

Another of those role transitions occurs when we change our employment status. One's work, career, or profession can and often does change or even disappear. Our generation has heard about "downsizing," a euphemism for being "terminated," "let go," "fired," or—in the words of the British—"sacked!" To me, the saddest words that Shakespeare ever wrote are, "Othello's occupation's gone." I recall such a situation during the time when printing became computerized and typesetting went the way of the horse-drawn buggy. A printing-house owner I knew had devoted a lifetime to building his business. When the changes in the industry began to occur, he saw himself as too old to change methods; he was probably too tired or perhaps too set in his ways to undergo a personal restructuring. To make such a changeover would have required tremendous energy, which I doubt he had. He closed his shop, let his employees go, and tried to settle into a life of retirement. He never succeeded because he was unable to let go of his profession, his ambition, his goals, and, most of all, something he could control. He could not separate his identity as a person from his identity in his business.

Whatever we hold onto so tenaciously may prove destructive. No matter how important work is to our personal identity and how much it contributes to society, it can become so consuming, demanding, and all-encompassing that it leaves no time, energy, or space for development into a broader and fuller personhood. For many people, their happiest and most productive years occur in the aftermath of some kind of job loss or retirement. To achieve such a positive result lies in one's ability to let go of what was in order to take up whatever can be. The Apostle Paul experienced a conversion that encompassed both his entire way of life and his personal identity. That conversion also involved his profession, his career, his calling. Think about what he left behind—the religion he knew from the cradle, his family about which we know little or nothing, and his clerical life in the order of Pharisees. We assume he also left behind a certain material prosperity. Pharisees were often

wealthy; he apparently had the luxury to travel to perse-
cute those he believed troubled his religion. Paul let go
of all such privilege. He devoted an entire section of his
letter to the church at Philippi to letting go of what is
past (Philippians 3:1–21). Paul said, "[T]his one thing I
do: forgetting what lies behind and straining forward to
what lies ahead, I press toward the goal for the prize of
the heavenly call of God in Christ Jesus" (Philippians
3:13b–14).

Each person's "goal" is different. In order to serve
God, to become full human beings, to mature in faith
and work, some of the weight, the past, and what is old
must be released. As we release what is no longer valuable and operative, those same attachments begin to
release us.

Letting Go and Our Physical Condition

Those who live long enough more likely than not will
experience an erosion of physical capabilities, stamina,
and function. Occasionally, an accident, disease, or some
other condition brings about a loss of physical function
suddenly or earlier than anticipated. Christopher Reeve,
a high-profile movie personality and ironically the star
of the film *Superman*, suffered a paralyzing horseback-
riding accident that has forever changed the course of
his life. Actor Michael J. Fox was struck by Parkinson's
disease; his career and personal life have also been
affected. An accident, a heart attack, a stroke, or a disease
can change dramatically what any of us is able to do.

Some, through therapy and personal will, fight to regain former function; many cannot in spite of their strong desire and even heroic efforts. These people face important decisions about how they will understand, interpret, and reconstruct their lives. Such understanding always grows out of one's personal value system.

Both Christopher Reeve and Michael J. Fox have turned their loss of physical strength and movement into advocacy. They use their celebrity status to articulate values of personhood that transcend their disabilities. They model ways to turn personal misfortune to public good.

Those who make the best adjustments to their new conditions or states of being find ways to let go of what they have obviously lost. I watched an excellent furniture maker gradually give up his tools as he lost his eyesight over a period of several years. He knew he could no longer see well enough to operate power machinery, take proper measurements, and carry out tasks that would result in additional beautiful reproductions for his home. He was able to let go of his hobby gracefully, with pride in what he had done; he refocused his activities in other directions. He filled the void with travel, service on various boards and committees of his church, vegetable gardening, and a very active social life. He became an inspiration to many people dealing with handicaps.

But even those who never experience debilitating accidents or diseases face that inevitable decline in physical well-being. Eyesight often diminishes, sometimes without hope of treatment. Not all hearing loss can be corrected with hearing devices. The aging process leaves many of us with restricted mobility. I suffer from a non-specific motor neuron disease, sometimes associated with Lou Gehrig's disease. I have no breathing or swallowing difficulties, but my legs and arms have lost muscle mass; I have difficulty walking very far and negotiating stairs. I often experience balance problems. Like many older people, I see things I once did and enjoyed doing and feel some sadness about my limitations, yet I try to focus less on what I have lost and more on what I still have.

My wife and I recently visited Boston for several days. Our agenda included visits to three art museums. After one day in the city, with the amount of walking required, my legs felt like rubber. The next day at the Boston Museum of Fine Arts my wife suggested I borrow a wheelchair. My first reaction was very negative. I decided, however, that no one there knew me, so I would try it. I later used wheelchairs at the other two museums. The experience helped me enjoy the artwork better than I could have otherwise; it also exposed my false pride and challenged me to use what was available for my mobility.

When major physical disabilities occur or a gradual loss of our physical capacities creeps up on us, much more is at stake than physical therapy and rehabilitation. Not just the physical body, but the whole person faces a new life. In order to let go emotionally of a physical function no longer possible, one must look again at the issue of self-worth. In a world that values people for what they can do, what they own, and what they look like, a physical disability may appear to devalue personhood. A previously healthy, active, successful man may be reduced in his own mind and in that of his culture to little more than an object of pity.

Letting go of vibrant health and certain skills requires more than an attitude of helpless acceptance. Christopher Reeve reported that soon after his fall he wanted to die. Instead, his family and friends, admirers and well-wishers helped him to tap his own inner strength. He has not given up hope of walking again, but he seems to have let go of the wholeness of body that he enjoyed before the accident. He has turned his energies to fundraising and to raising the national consciousness about nerve damage.

The conscious act of letting these capabilities go may well open the way to the birth of some new interest, ability, or gift we might not have known about otherwise. The famous violinist Itzhak Perlman commented that, had he not been stricken with a crippling disease, he might have spent all his time playing baseball instead of practicing music. He might have been another Mark McGwire, but the world of music would have been the poorer.

Letting Go and Forgiveness

Atop a long list of excess baggage, we read the word "sin"—our own, both personal and corporate sins in which we have been complicitous, as well as sins committed against us. The psalmist places sin in the context of divine love.

For as the heavens are high above the earth,
so great is his steadfast love toward those who fear him;
as far as the east is from the west,
so far he removes our transgressions from us.
(Psalm 103:11–12)

God may have removed our sins, forgiven us, and
washed us clean of them; our memories, however, tend
to be such that we hold onto the awful awareness of
what we have done and what we have left undone. At
some point in time, at a juncture in our experience, we
can do what God has done—forgive ourselves, amend
our way of life, and let go of all sin that is past. Perhaps
the most difficult person to forgive is oneself; surely, the
most liberating act is accepting God's forgiveness and
letting go of what we have done and cannot undo.

Awareness of our sins inevitably raises feelings of two
possible kinds of guilt. Neurotic guilt has no reality in
fact. A mother may feel guilty when her child has an
accident, yet she did nothing to allow the child to get in
harm's way. Neurotic guilt should be acknowledged and
released. Legitimate guilt, on the other hand, is based on
reality. The good news of Jesus says that if we confess
our sins, God forgives us. God separates that sin from us
"as far as the east is from the west." We, too, must let
those sins go.

Just as liberating is releasing the sins of others who
have wronged us, especially those we love. Jesus surely
recognized the connection between our own sins and the
sins committed against us. "Forgive us our trespasses, as

we forgive those who trespass against us." How much easier to nurse old grievances, hold onto grudges, dismiss or devalue those who have harmed us, hold them in contempt! How satisfying to wish harm, or at least no good fortune, for our enemies. Families become fractured because some members hang onto and nurse old wounds. Offices, factories, and other workplaces become tense and unpleasant because of real or perceived injustices. Churches seethe in turmoil and often split because sins, mistakes, and differing opinions become permanent institutional fixtures.

The beginning point in the forgiveness of others may be written in that same psalm: "[S]o far he removes our transgressions from us" (Psalm 103:12). How easy it is to claim God's forgiveness for ourselves but to deny it or resent it for those who have harmed us. Many psalmists spoke openly about the pain inflicted by others. In fact, the Psalter is replete with references to enemies, foes, adversaries, and those who sabotage. The poet of Psalm 27 opens by verbalizing his struggle with fear of evildoers; later he refers specifically to those who have forsaken him. (Psalm 27:10). In Psalm 55, the lament concerns not an enemy but a companion, a close friend with whom the psalmist had even gone to the Temple. A similar and poignant reference to a family division makes the writer of Psalm 69 an outcast from his family— perhaps because of religious convictions (verse 8). Fear, loneliness, and anger characterize many of the psalms in which enemies are a primary focus, but they contain few references to the one who had been wronged offering forgiveness to the transgressors. Only much later in biblical history, particularly in the ministry of Jesus, do we see forgiveness of others emphasized. Our experience demonstrates how damaging the inability or unwillingness to forgive others can be to anyone and everyone.

Unwillingness to forgive others poisons us, festers, and becomes a spreading disease in our community. Rigid, angry, and unforgiving people cast a dark pall wherever they go. They tend to isolate themselves and then wonder about the absence of true and intimate friends. Such people tend to be more susceptible to illness, to serious physical diseases, and to emotional imbalances. Should we be surprised that Jesus associated illness and infirmity with sin? He was far wiser than those who would dismiss that connection as first-century naïveté. An experienced physician is said to have advised his son just out of medical school: "Before you ask them what they have been eating, ask what has been eating them!"

Anger may be at the heart of "what's eating them." With its roots in a sense of being wronged or of not getting one's own way, it may be the most silent and destructive of all emotions. Everyone gets angry or should get angry; it is a natural and healthy emotion. Some, however, become perpetually angry people. Unresolved, unmitigated, and relentless anger causes damaging results, including high blood pressure, migraine headaches, heart attacks, cancer, mental illness, and social isolation. Anger gone to seed opens the door to evil entering and controlling the angry person. Such damage to the self defies description, but damage to the angry person's workplace, family, neighborhood, and church go far beyond the mere hurt feelings that result from an occasional confrontation. The angry person leaves flotsam and jetsam in his or her wake and often dies prematurely. Such angry people are at the top of the list of those who need to be forgiven; those they have damaged may need to distance themselves from such destructive behavior. If those who are angry choose not to be redeemed, they must not be permitted to continue to plague those they have harmed. Part of forgiveness may include simply moving away from them, physically and emotionally.

As we consider forgiveness of self and others and the letting go of sins—our own and those of others who have sinned against us—we will inevitably face the issue of which comes first. Is forgiveness of ourselves and others possible only after we have let go of the sin? Must we first forgive in order to be able to let go of the sin? Or are forgiveness and letting go two sides of the same coin? We have all heard someone say, "I forgive, but I can't forget." Memory is indeed powerful. What we have done and what has been done to us sometimes marks us for life. The scars do not fade very much with time. Such is our humanity.

Surely each of us can find the grace of release in our own time and sequence. My own most recent experiences led me first to letting go. Forgiveness of myself and/or another person seems less difficult when I am not pre-occupied by memories, visions, nightmares, images, and symbols of the sins committed. The importance of

Compline at the end of the day or at the end of a longer period lies in the very act of letting go in order that a peaceful rest may follow.

Those errors I have committed and for which I have asked forgiveness may resurface from time to time. I may recall the wrongs done to me on an anniversary date, in a fleeting memory, or in a chance meeting with an offending party. Letting go and forgiveness do not take away every memory or erase every scar. That is why I need daily Compline: as a reminder that we let some things go, we have been forgiven, and we have tendered forgiveness.

A sixth-century evening hymn includes a stanza that says,

> Lest we beset by doubt and strife,
> forget your blessed gift of life,
> and anguish and in mind distressed,
> be crushed by guilt,
> by sin oppressed.
> (from "O Blest Creator, source of light")

Another hymn, "Most Holy God, the Lord of heaven," contains the request, "Free us from bonds of blinding sin, and guide us on our path to you."

Finally, one of my favorite hymns, which is often sung as a canon (in "rounds"), asks this:

> Forgive me, Lord, for thy dear Son,
> the ill that I this day have done;

that with the world, myself, and thee,
I, ere I sleep, at peace may be.
(from "All praise to thee, my God, this night")

Note the theme of freedom as the expression of the ability to let go and be liberated. Perhaps as we ask forgiveness for our own sins, God then forgives us and we are able to let them go. For the sins of others against us, we can both let go and eventually forgive. Ultimately, forgiving and being forgiven are bound together. At the end of the day or the week or after a long and protracted conflict, real peace and rest come only to us who are unburdened of all sin—our own, and the sins of others against us.

In a difficult conversation with his disciples, Jesus proposed that we forgive our enemies, not seven times, but seventy times seven (Matthew 18:21–22). If we read that instruction as a commandment, we carry a weight of unbearable expectation. If, however, we read that teaching as a promise—you will be able to forgive seventy times seven—we accept these words of Jesus as a gift: God empowers us to do the godly thing.

One caveat about forgiveness and accountability, however, is that forgiveness does not let us off the hook. Each of us remains responsible for what we have done. When possible, we can attempt to make right what we have done wrong. Forgiveness never lets the sinner off the hook. When we sin we can accept the consequences and, whenever possible, seek to make amends.

Letting Go and Grief

Any and every word about letting go of what we have lost—and the grief attached to it—demands extreme care. Bookstore shelves and publishers' lists bulge with personal accounts of losses and heart-rending stories of grief. Some of these books—with their pious interpretations of tragedies and their suggestions of formulaic patterns of how to deal with them—offend grieving people. Patterns do exist, but so do griefs that seem to fit no formula. Each grief is actually unique to itself.

Some losses are so severe that the issue becomes not so much our desire to let go of our grief; the problem is that the loss itself will not release us. I speak here more about the tragic and unexpected death of a loved one and/or of a violent act against someone, not about the multitude of other more predictable losses we sustain and their patterned processes of recovery.

I remember vividly the slow death of a very old woman. She lay in a coma for several years. One day her daughter asked me to visit with her and her mother. While I was there, the daughter spoke directly to her mother. She told her how much she loved her and what a positive influence the mother had been upon her. Then she acknowledged her mother's long illness and struggle to remain with her. Now, said the daughter, she was prepared to let her go. We prayed together and I tried to affirm what the daughter had said to her mother. The old woman died that night. Because the daughter had been willing to let go of her mother, her comatose mother must have heard her and seemed to find the will to let go of her life.

As grievous as they may be, such good-byes are appropriate, liberating, and even essential. Not all of us allow our parents, our friends, or even our aged spouses to go so clearly or as early. In some cases, the release does not take place for years. I am told of a college student whose mother died while the young woman was in high school. She remained angry with her mother for several years because she felt her mother had abandoned her. (Remember, our interpretations of losses are not always rational.) For several years she held on to every memory, even her mother's clothing and personal effects, and she kept them just as they had been when her mother died. One day, at the encouragement of her counselor, she went to the cemetery. In a long and tearful conversation, she told her mother good-bye. When the young woman let go, her anger began to melt away and positive memories began to take its place.

But what about the family of a teenager killed in a car accident? Or a murdered loved one? Or a child who dies of a dreaded disease? Would anyone dare offer any advice to families in such pain? Do their griefs fit a pattern or a formula? Who even begins to comprehend what they have gone through and what they will suffer in the future? The best gift to such a person may be the gift of a caring and silent presence. The most that can be said, gently and tearfully, is that the loved one and the searing grief of those who remain might by grace be entrusted to God. Such pain of loss grips these sufferers that years later, the death seems like yesterday.

I sat with a woman in her eighties and listened as she told me about the tragic and accidental death of her younger son. She plowed through every painful detail, each element of her tale relayed in perfect order. Tears flowed down her cheeks. I asked her how long her son had been gone. "Sixty years," she answered. To her it seemed like sixty minutes or sixty days.

Oh, if only such losses could be given over to God, such loved ones committed to heaven. But these tragedies grip with iron jaws; memory keeps the edges torn and raw. Those of us who care about people who have suffered such losses simply stand and watch most of the time, without a legitimate clue to the depth of their pain. Jesus was able to say to the Father, "Into thy hands I commend my spirit." Those who die by violence and pestilence seldom have even the time to pray such words, and those they leave behind may, in the words of Saint Paul, only sigh like the Spirit who makes intercession for them (Romans 8:26). No words adequately express the most intense grief. We have only those guttural groans.

How can letting go be possible in these circumstances? How can those who experience such enormous loss find liberation from the intensity of the pain while continuing to honor the memory, spirit, and presence of the one who died? Perhaps giving a loved one to God would comfort those left behind, easing their pain with the knowledge that in God's presence those who die continue to grow in grace, peace, and service.

Fortunately, time really does make a difference. While the sense of physical presence diminishes, the spiritual presence of the person lost remains. The torn and ragged edges are always there but, as one parent told me, they become "a little less jagged with time." I have also observed that letting go cannot be separated from a sense of being let go. The intensity of grief gradually loosens its hold on those left behind—yet it never turns them loose completely.

The Role of Memory

Those who grieve the loss of anything or anyone always deal with memory. The human mind often seems like the world's most powerful computer, storing everything we have ever seen, heard, or done. The right stimulus at the right moment calls to mind and heart something we may not have thought about in years. Sometimes, however, we are able by intention to let go of whatever has held us in the grips of grief, be it the loss of a person or our sins and failures or a former status and role. Each of us has some choice, even if memories prevent total release. The memories attached to the circumstances, situations, and people may fade a bit with time, but they will never completely go away. Nor do we want them to leave us completely.

Memory can serve as a blessing, or it can damage us like a curse. In a short story entitled "Grandparenting," John Updike has one of the characters say, "Nobody belongs to us except in memory" (*The Afterlife and Other*

Stories [New York: Fawcett, 1996]). If we agree, we might also say that no thing belongs to us forever, except in memory. As for our experiences, they are truly our own, both in fact and in memory. Each of us, therefore, has a choice about how to use memory. Memories of wrongs done to us and kept alive and vivid tend to turn us to bitterness; this bitterness pushes others away from us. Memories of failures, sins, and mistakes can be nursed and rehearsed until guilt clouds everything, even the image of God. Overblown memories of past achievements might prevent us from entering a new and bright future.

Memory can also serve us well. Memories of a lost loved one can bring us pleasure and even joy. I have listened to families at holiday meals tell stories and anecdotes about one whose place at the table is empty, but whose place in the hearts of each family member is still very much occupied. Memory also serves us well when the mistakes we have made and the transitions we have navigated remind us how to be and do better than before.

We cannot control memory, but we can choose what use we will make of it. Positive recollections can honor, inspire, teach, and encourage; bitter memories can provide an excuse not to let go, forgive, heal, or move on with our lives.

Letting Go: Some How-To's

When we face the need to let go of whatever we have chosen to release or to move into whatever transition life imposes upon us, we may discover that the process requires thinking, planning, and help. The first step involves separating what we have been holding onto from what has been holding onto us. In many of our most severe losses, we discover that when we begin to release from within ourselves our grief, pain, failure, sin, injustice, person, position, or condition, those losses begin to loosen their hold upon us. In the process of letting go, the torn and jagged edges begin to be less sharp and searing.

I suggest four ways you can help yourself let go. First, *recognize that letting go most often requires some act of will, a conscious and intentional effort.* I have long admired those who sustain brutal and bitter changes with heroic courage and effort. Obviously, the greater the loss or injury, the more difficulty we have turning our faces to the wind and marching on, and the longer it requires to get moving. Nevertheless, prolonged self-pity, anger, or bitterness simply intensify our pain and may even drive us into deeper despair and isolation.

I was blessed to develop a friendship with an older woman after she lost her husband. She did not drive an automobile, but she decided to go to lunch with someone at least once a week. She paid for lunch and the person she invited drove them to a restaurant. She tried to fill her emptiness with friends and table conversation. I was not surprised at how she moved into a positive life without her husband; she had always been forward in her thinking and socially active. Her loss was enormous and her pain was torturous, but she refused to give in to it.

Like memories, we have little control of the emotions that accompany great loss and significant change; we do have some control over what we do with those emotions. We can choose to harbor bitterness, anger, and loneliness, not only when we have suffered because of injustice but also when we have suffered from life's randomness. Alternatively, we can choose a path toward forgiveness, release, and recreating our lives. The positive approach will always be difficult for some and may initially appear impossible for others; the length of time required will vary from person to person. Over time, desire and effort can lighten the burden, replacing an old way of life with a new one.

Second, *embrace what is new, different, and even partially unknown*. Every major loss guarantees newness, not simply because of the emotions it arouses, but also because an empty space demands to be filled. When we can no longer do something we have always done, such as a professional function, parenting, a hobby, or a sport, we have an opportunity to do something we have never done before. The loss of a loved one opens the doors to relationships with others. The empty nest, for example, means that parents who have devoted much of their energy to childrearing are free to direct some of those resources and compassions elsewhere.

Whatever we find or create to fill the voids may prove to make letting go and healing come about more quickly and smoothly. I think about a woman diagnosed with a debilitating disease in which her body began to atrophy. Her physician suggested a move to a warmer climate. In the midst of the struggle with her illness and the pain of moving far from her family and friends, she found a place in the Southwest United States. She consciously embraced her own physical limitations and her mortality, but she determined to embrace whatever new experiences and people would come her way. She soon found a church, a health club, new neighbors, and a way of contributing to her new life by watching out for people in need through telephone calls and by sending greeting cards.

J. B. Phillips translates the words of Saint Paul to the church at Rome this way: "The whole creation is on tiptoe to see the wonderful sight of the sons (and daughters) of God coming into their own" (Romans 8:19). A solid case may be made from both Scripture and experience that suffering that comes about as a result of transitions can and often does lead toward spiritual development. Such a change may come at very high price. The darkness into which we are plunged may render the future most uncertain and frightening; however, the newness we embrace can also help ease the pain.

I think sometimes about the most difficult periods of my own life and would do almost anything to avoid another such experience. Each one almost destroyed me. I considered suicide after my academic failure and during the transition our family went through. I came close to becoming nonfunctional when I left the Baptist church. At the same time, I readily, albeit sometimes reluctantly, admit that out of those fiery ordeals I have emerged as a better, more compassionate, more complete person. I have grown in mind, emotion, and spirit. I venture to say that those who know me best would quickly agree. Surely I am not alone in this kind of transformation.

Four days after I completed my examinations for ordination in the Episcopal Church, I received a call from the rector of the church I now serve. He asked me to come and talk with him about working as a second clergy. In the course of our discussion, he said that he sensed my brokenness would lead to growth and a substantive ministry. And so it has been.

Experience, my own and those of others I have watched, suggests very strongly that spiritual development occurs more readily and more frequently during or following painful transitions. When life goes well and we seem to be in control of everything, God may be an afterthought. When change threatens our sense of well-being and order, we may cry out to God with real urgency. When life hammers away at us, when nothing seems to be nailed down, when the future is actually up for grabs, God gets our attention. In such times, we find it easy to reexamine priorities, question our faith, and gaze into the depths of ourselves. People who have experienced blackness tend to love the light. When there is no song, we learn to appreciate the simplest melody. God uses our chaotic lives, our questions, our darkness, and our pain as windows into our souls.

A man told me that when he entered a forced retirement from work he loved, he learned to pray. Always before, he explained, he did all the talking. In his sadness, he learned to listen to the Bible, to God's Spirit, to the people of God, and to his own truest self. Again, the sun that hardens the clay melts the wax!

Third, *rely on community*. Letting go best occurs with the support of those who know us best, who journey through the hard times with us, who listen, pray, advise when asked, and show us what tearful eyes and broken hearts may miss without their help. A woman who lost a child in death told me that the most helpful gift people gave her was the gift of a brief visit or telephone call simply to say she was on their minds and in their hearts.

Of course, the danger always exists that some will say and do something that makes the road more difficult. Simplistic answers, inappropriate questions, moralizing, sermonizing, or advising only add to the difficulty. Such is the risk of community. But the value of those who are most sensitive and wise far outweighs the well-intended bungling of others. I believe from my own experience that those who care for us most make letting go of grief, loss, and pain more possible and allow it to happen more quickly; they seem willing and able to take some of our misery from us.

Finally, *rely on God's grace*. Letting go of sin, injustice, robust health, role and status, place, and loved ones, occurs for many of us with the help of grace. How else could we forgive others except that God forgives us? In fact, Jesus' admonition that we forgive seems to be less a command than a promise, an empowerment. Through Jesus, God tells us that what we are asked to do, and we will be given the grace to do it. How else can we let go of loved ones unless we have hope that they are in the presence of God? How else can we fall from places of influence and prestige and survive unless we know that in the eyes of God our worth is not determined by what we do but by God's love for us?

It is less difficult to leave a place where we have lived for a long time when we realize that God's people are also in the place we are going. We can release our sons and daughters more readily into a very big world when we remind ourselves that God goes with them. Because God has already granted us grace, the people of God are able to let go and to turn toward the newness we must inevitably embrace.

But what of those losses and injustices that will not let us go completely? Saint Paul can help us here. He referred to a "thorn in the flesh," which he believed had been given to him as a preventative against undue pride. Based on his comments in the letter to the church in Corinth, some believe that it was a rather ugly eye disease. Whatever it was, the Apostle had prayed that this "thorn in the flesh" would be removed, but God answered: "My grace is sufficient for you, for power is made perfect in weakness" (2 Corinthians 12:9). I doubt that one person should make such a statement to another; I am equally certain that anyone held in the grip of some pain, loss, or injustice may interpret the situation as at least a means of some form of faith development. I have asked myself many times out of my own pain, "How has this changed you?" I would not, however, appreciate others' attempting to make such interpretations on my behalf.

Letting Go: From Emptiness into Transition

Saint Paul's hymn to the Incarnation—Philippians 2:5–11—sings about Jesus who had been in the "form" of God but emptied himself and took on the "form" of a servant, being born in human likeness. We know very little about the thirty-year span between his human birth and his divinely anointed mission. We might say that these years were necessary to in-form this new form. If Jesus became truly human, childhood and the learning necessary for emerging maturity demanded that long, slow process. Between the letting go of the form of divinity and assuming his messianic mission, many changes took place.

Jesus grew as every human child, became acculturated, increased in stature, in wisdom, and in favor with God and with those who knew him. He was tested in every way that we are tested. He was obedient to his parents. Whatever he was and however he was before his birth, he became fully human. We can only imagine what he let go in order to become like we are. Such is the Incarnation: as much a letting go as a taking upon.

So it is with all experiences of release or letting go. In some sense, especially when we let go of a person, a condition, a status, an opinion, or an object of importance, we experience an emptiness, a vacuum, a hollowness prior to moving on to the next stage of our new lives. In the process, each of us becomes a different person; the alteration may be great or small, but our identity is affected.

The self-emptying of our grief and pain corresponds with that of Jesus only in that we also must let go of what has been in order to become what we will be.

Our initial response to one of these life-altering experiences may be searing grief, hurt, resentment, feelings of failure, despair, and loss—these emotions may overwhelm us and cause us to become obsessed, dominated, and controlled by what we have done or by what has happened to us. We may tend to forget to take care of the house and yard, neglect to schedule routine medical examinations, or fail to honor family events such as birthdays. As we return to our routines, however, we begin to release what has held us in a painful grasp; we realize that a certain emptiness has developed. This may be quite different from the empty house after a son or daughter has gone to college or to a job away from home; this emptiness has been created by an emotional response to a powerful situation. As the intensity of emotion lessens, feelings of depletion creep in.

During the most recent, particularly painful time in my own life, for several months I could only sit and work jigsaw puzzles because I could not concentrate on anything else. I sat at the table and stared at colors and shapes, often through tears. As I began to let go of the pain or the pain began to let go of me, I found myself wandering about the house and through the day wondering what to do next—or first. I experienced an emptiness that I could not explain and did not know exactly how to fill. I was certain, however, that it would be filled.

I was living in a kind of in-between period, like a trapeze flyer. Imagine the woman (the flyer) swinging back
and forth on one trapeze and the man (the catcher) on
the other. High above the floor with no net beneath, the
flyer lets go and the circus-goers suspend their breathing
until the catch is made—then comes the applause.

Even while I was letting go—flying through the air
as it were—I had begun the hard, impatient work of
waiting. I had known months earlier that a period of
waiting would follow the period of letting go, but I
could not have predicted how empty the transition
between the two would be. This dual process reminded
me of the accelerator and clutch problem many of us
had when we were learning to drive a car with a standard
transmission. The movement of each pedal had to be
coordinated with the other or we would kill the motor
and be forced to begin again.

I have often told widows and widowers that the loss
of a lifelong mate may be the most difficult of all losses.
Nothing will ever be the same. Yet life can be good
again, provided they do the work of reinventing their
lives in the aftermath of so great a transition. Such a profound life change demands careful attention to the
emptiness and to the bridge ahead.

The man who has built a successful company, influ-
enced hundreds of people, and enjoyed prominence in
his community will be markedly different when he no
longer sits in the executive's seat. Whether he makes the
transition because of declining or sudden loss of health,
the comfort of his prosperity, or simply by his own

choice, his life will take on a different shape, either by his own making or of its own weight. How will he fill those twelve working hours each day? How will he fill the void in professional status that will diminish with each passing year?

The professional athlete shares something of that story. At forty years of age, what has been central to his or her life since childhood is no longer possible. Physical skills have eroded with age and time. The cameras seek out another hero. The same can be said of most public figures who make the transition from prominence to private citizenship.

To a lesser degree, every one of us who undergoes a transition brought about by what we let go—by accident or by choice—faces for a time some kind of emptiness or vacuum pointing to the need to reconstruct a different life. The young woman mentioned earlier must replace her anger toward her dead mother with something else. Parents must find a new focus when they are no longer needed by sons and daughters who have left home and set out on their own. The ex-professional athlete must redefine a life out of the limelight and find something else to live for. The bereaved may need to transfer some of the love they once heaped upon one who has died to some other person or to some other thing.

When our lives take a major turn and we are forced to let go of something or someone—or if we have chosen to do so—the feelings of emptiness may continue for weeks and even months. The future may be as invisible as a distant object in the fog. We may feel as if we are wandering in a wilderness, caught in a maze, lost after a storm. Yet, as we have discussed, such feelings of emptiness might well be a necessary condition. Just because nothing seems to be happening may not mean that nothing is happening.

Letting go is seldom complete at the time we begin to wait for what lies ahead. In fact, some of the letting go never ends completely. Even the letting go demands a certain waiting, a recognition of process. Those experiencing severe grief eventually experience days without tears; they think to themselves, "I haven't cried a single time today." Later, those recovering from grief experience days when they laugh aloud, saying to themselves, "That is the first time in ages I have done that."

Similarly, we may experience the fading of our anger about an injustice toward us until we think the resentment is completely gone. But then, quite suddenly, something triggers memory and we may feel a sharp twinge of anger, or we may even express that anger verbally toward whomever or whatever is nearby. Some object, calendar date, story, voice in a crowd, photograph, or memory brings back to us what we have been trying to let go. The tears may come or we may withdraw from activities for a while. What seems like an emotional vacuum is never completely empty. The pain may never be gone completely; nevertheless, pain, loss, grief, failure, or absence will soften as the vacuum begins to fill with new people, events, projects, and dreams.

The time of active waiting is marked by hope and by a solid faith that life may not be the same, but that life can be good again—and it will be. I suspect that the most important realization occurring in the letting-go process may be that of coming to grips with our mortality. The Compline hour of the Daily Office helps us to let go of the day and many of the events and experiences of the day—including our failures and losses. The act of retiring for the night, taking to our beds, and falling asleep serves in some ways as a voluntary dying. The Scriptures often refer to death as sleeping.

The people of God believe, however, that the metaphor of sleep cannot be separated from the metaphor of rising with the sun, a kind of resurrection. Jesus said of Lazarus, "Our friend has fallen asleep, but I am going there to awaken him" (John 11:11). Saint Paul uses the metaphor of sleep to address the issue of resurrection (I Corinthians 15:51 and I Thessalonians 4:14); these references in various translations use the words for sleep and death interchangeably.

The Compline prayers ask for peace in order that sleep may truly become rest. When, through prayer and acts of our own will, we are able to let go of our most severe pain, sleep tends to be more restful and renewing. When we are most troubled, sleep tends to be fitful, restless, and marked by disturbing dreams. Restful sleep, on the other hand, allows an emptying of ourselves and what troubles us in the hope and faith that our lives will in some sense begin to be transformed and filled during the process of our waiting.

CHAPTER TWO

Waiting

The vacuum! Weeks and months of letting go, interior good-byes, some smoothing of the jagged edges, occasional laughter, fewer tears, the first hints of being able to forgive injustice and live with questions that cannot be answered—but what now? Where to from here? How does one deal with the vacuum; how does one fill it? We may have been dragged kicking and screaming into our transitions or we may have chosen them with great excitement; nevertheless, we inevitably leave much behind and those losses hurt. Having dealt with the hurt, we must now begin the construction of whatever we will become.

Throughout my years in ministry, I have counseled many people dealing with severe changes and the accompanying losses. I have consistently verbalized what certainly passes as a truism: "Your life will never again be the same! *But*, that does not mean it cannot be good." Much of what life becomes depends on our own desire and will; much also lies within mystery, especially to those who are open to such gifts, and comes about as a surprise.

The period of letting go tends to be filled with intense feelings, emotional outbursts, agitation, and even furious activity by which we try to cover or avoid the intensity. When raw nerves begin to heal and the jagged edges of pain become a little less sharp, we can feel ourselves moving into a different state of being. The period of waiting carries with it a gradual calming, a more reflective spirit, questioning that is more open and less accusatory. However, while we are waiting for the healing to begin, as I pointed out in chapter one, we may feel as if we are living in a vacuum. That can be frightening and we may not know what we are supposed to be doing.

We begin with a willingness to embrace the silence, the emptiness, and especially the uncertainty. Such an embrace tends to run against the grain of our culture. No less an authority than Dr. Seuss comments on the subject of waiting in his book, *Oh, the Places You'll Go.* A youngster starts out on the journey of adventure toward greatness and fulfillment, but along the way he is stalled by an unexpected "slump," stuck in what the author calls "a most useless place—The Waiting Place."

We tend to experience silence and inactivity as passivity, wasted time, irresponsibility. We use the expression "killing time" almost profanely. Time is perhaps our most important asset and yet we often treat it as a throwaway commodity. The Quakers tell a story about a visitor to a worship service. The visitor seats himself next to a woman of the congregation. After a long period of silence, he whispers to her, "When does the service begin?" She replies rather impatiently, "The service begins when worship has ended." In other words, the fact that nothing seems to be happening does not necessarily mean that nothing is happening.

Impatience may cause us to close our eyes and hearts to surprises, serendipity, new or deeper relationships, and opportunities for creativity. If we allow it to do so, woundedness enables us to be quiet and listen, to open our inner eyes and see. Perhaps the period when we begin to emerge from the most intense pain becomes the time when our sight and hearing reach their finest levels of sensitivity. We can see what we have never seen before, hear what our ears could not hear until our lives became sensitized; the very nerve endings of our souls rise to the surface. We will neither see nor hear on such a deep level if we throw our lives into a frenzy of activity in order to evade the reality of our injured or otherwise changed selves.

Withdrawing into a shell of self-pity or making ourselves sick with depression is easier than waiting and listening. The story of Elijah serves as a powerful example. After his greatest victory, Jezebel threatens his life. Elijah runs and hides in a cave, surely symbolic of his fear and depression. But God comes to him and asks a deceptively simple question: "What are you doing here?" (I Kings 19:1–21). Had Elijah gone to the famous mountain to wait for God's direction, for God's voice, or had he gone to reflect upon and assess his situation, would God have faulted him? He had no legitimate excuse for withdrawing into fear and self-pity. His faith in God and in himself failed him in the sunlight of his greatest victory!

Embracing the silence and enduring the period of waiting requires that we give up the desire for our pain to pass quickly. The loss of our pain may actually thwart the more creative and productive uses of suffering. To hurry past the pain may be to hurry past opportunity. Calm and patient waiting, active waiting, may open us and those sharing our pain to the increased sensitivity required to see and hear the mystery of what we will become.

It bears repeating: Whatever we will become requires stillness, with no agenda and no timetable. The basis of such waiting lies in the foundation of Jesus' promise of presence: "I am with you always, even to the end of the age" (Matthew 28:20). Nevertheless, God's promise is not always self-evident, nor does it always manifest itself in ways we expect. Therefore, we wait for God's presence to be known to us. Such waiting is not passive. Neither is it the opposite of impulsive or compulsive activity. Nor does such waiting give us license to relinquish responsibility for ourselves, for those we love, or for our daily duties.

Waiting in and after great pain, however, may provide us with gifts, answers, and directions. Perhaps the initial and most daunting gift is the exhilarating and even frightening opportunity to discover ourselves in ways we never knew, to embrace even our darkest side, long suppressed or denied. Loss and attendant pain tend to expose shadow aspects of who we are; the loss and pain sometimes force us to confront these aspects and even embrace them. They are part of what it means to be fully human.

Ideally, we will gain a sense of the evil within ourselves as well as our God-given goodness, without which the dark or the shadow side of ourselves would have no positive meaning.

The shadows, the depths, the realities about ourselves that we have cleverly pushed deeper and deeper and deftly hid from ourselves and others often carry with them the element of surprise as well as of mystery. One aspect of that surprise is the discovery that our vulnerability will not destroy us or repel others who discover we are not really perfect. Instead, that vulnerability helps us become someone who welcomes others to share our common pain and our common humanity.

The words of one of Spain's finest philosophers, Miguel De Unamuno, are seldom far from my mind and my experience:

> I am convinced that we should solve many things if we all went out into the streets and uncovered our griefs, which perhaps would prove to be but one sole common grief, and join together in beweeping them and crying aloud to the heavens and calling upon God. And this, even though God should not hear us; but he would hear us. The chiefest sanctity of a temple is that it is a place to which men go to weep in common. (*The Tragic Sense of Life* [New York: Dover, 1954], p. 17)

Why would we want to give such public expression to personal sorrow, to dredge up our shadow side, and to expose our demons? We do so precisely because we are human. We face our pain honestly and examine our shadow side simply because they are part of who we are and what we are. The result of their discovery, or rediscovery, need not lead to depression and self-loathing, but rather to a greater patience with ourselves. I believe that most of us are far too hard on ourselves; some of us try to cover over everything we dislike about ourselves—even self-loathing—by meticulous, compulsive perfectionism. As a result, an even greater dislike of ourselves develops as we fail to live up to our own unrealistic standards. We find ourselves in a vicious circle, like a dog chasing its own tail.

A similar attitude toward others leaches through our own unrealistic standards: we may become judgmental, critical, contemptuous, harsh, and sometimes mean-spirited when others fail to live up to our expectations. Loss and accompanying pain, at least for a time, intensify self-criticism and may move us toward bitterness against anyone or anything we believe has contributed to our pain.

When we begin to let go of what we have lost, say good-bye, and even become grateful that we at least had for a time what we lost, then we are then able to look more deeply into ourselves. In the process, we can begin to embrace our full humanity—the persona or that role we have wanted to play—as well as our fears, insecurities, and all manner of sins. By its very nature, waiting allows these realities to re-emerge—those we think are positive and some we think are negative. If they do not emerge, we cannot see them, own them, deal with them, or allow them to instruct us. To embrace them because they are a real part of who we are renders us vulnerable, but in that vulnerability we learn compassion for ourselves as well as for others who experience loss, failure, and pain.

Vulnerability, compassion, empathy, and understanding lead us through the pain of our own losses, out from behind the facades we have constructed for ourselves, into relationships with others who also know what it means to have lost something or someone. Waiting forces us to give up some control, some power, and to allow brokenness to become a teacher, a priest, and even the voice of God's Spirit. Such vulnerability opens doorways to trust, intimacy, and joy in our relationships with others.

One of the great lessons we can learn from our most painful experiences is that we have control of much less than we had previously thought. Disease, accidents, aging, social change, and death come about willy-nilly, and we have very little control over these events and processes. Yet, by acknowledging them, by embracing the suffering they impose, and by consciously waiting for their reality to settle into our full consciousness, we allow them to be instructive at least, formative at best. Picasso is credited with having said, "Life breaks everyone, but some become strong in the broken places." The area in which a bone is fractured tends to become stronger in that place than before the break. However, the strengthening process requires time. So does the process of becoming and being fully human, embracing every aspect of who we are, "warts and all." The waiting place is far from a "most useless place"—if we do not turn it into a hiding place.

I have found the letting-go process to be the most difficult, the most intense, and the most painful. The waiting part proved not to be so difficult, which surprised me. I am still in my own waiting time, the time when we are still tender from the pain of what we have left, yet at a point in which we know we have turned it loose. We wait because we are not clear about what lies ahead. Perhaps we have moved to a new place, a new community, a new job, but we have not yet discovered our new role. We may no longer be there, but neither are we fully here. When I left my church and denomination, I did not know what work I would do; I had few ideas about how I would use my abilities. Some of the fear of being no longer useful and the anxiety about my financial future spent itself during the letting-go time.

I had explored several employment possibilities in the secular world, but I realized that these would not be fulfilling for me. I was reminded repeatedly that I am at heart a parish minister: such ministry is my calling and no amount of broadening the definition of "ministry" worked. When I turned my face again to the work I know and love and let go of much of my insecurity and fear, I was able gradually to move into the waiting place that became for me a comfortable place. I entered into conversation with bishops and clergy of the Episcopal Church in my area and placed myself at their disposal. I asked of them only three things: that I be permitted to study for examinations without returning to seminary, that I remain in my present residence, and that the time process for ordination be compressed as much as the canons of the church would allow. From that point on I resolved to ask no questions of them, to seek no place of employment in the church, and to wait for what God may have been doing already in my life. (Parenthetically, and a bit ahead of my story, I was ordained to the Episcopal ministry just over twenty months out of my Baptist career.) I resolved to enter this period of waiting while the process unfolded. I was not inactive, nor was I aggressively pursuing anything.

For the first time ever, I had no specific plan, no agenda other than to continue my gradual healing from loss and grief and to prepare myself for whatever ministry I could do. Some anxiety, yes. Some fearfulness and uncertainty, yes. Some residual depression, yes. At the same time hope, enthusiasm, humor, and joyfulness began to return. One of the best gifts I received at this time was an Emily Dickinson poem sent to me by a seminary professor who had experienced the same kind of loss, only in the academic community.

> Hope is the thing with feathers
> That perches in the soul,
> And sings the tune without the words,
> And never stops at all.

The gift of hope, the gift of calm!

Between Easter and Pentecost, the disciples of Jesus were never far from my thoughts. Imagine those followers who, in their idealism, left almost everything to participate in the coming reign of God. Their hope shattered almost as quickly as a clay jar dropped on the pavement. Jesus was dead, then risen from death, and then sporadically among them for several weeks. His instructions to them were limited to some vague commission about telling a story to the world; the assignment was far from clear or complete. He also instructed them to wait in Jerusalem (Acts 1:7–8).

The waiting part must surely have been the hard part. These early Christians waited only a few weeks, but they waited in what must have been enormous and intense pain, uncertainty, insecurity, and fear. They waited even when they could easily have returned to the security of their former lives. I, too, wondered if I could return to my former life. Returning to what once was, however, was not possible, so I chose to wait quietly but not without some effort to fill the vacuum. I knew I would give five months to reading and preparation for Episcopal ordination examinations, but this involved working only four to six hours a day. I had never in my life worked so few hours. If I chose to wait to see what the church would become for me and I to the church, and if I chose to wait for God's nudgings, I could not wait in a vacuum. I set four objectives. First, I knew I wanted to wait in God's presence; therefore, *worship* would be a major component for the months to come. Second, I felt great need in my life for *community*. I could not wait alone, but I would wait in the company of those who would encourage me but also hold me accountable. Third, I knew at some time in the process I would be forced to venture out, *test deeper waters,* and place myself in positions of risk in order to discover what I would become. Finally, I knew the waiting would give way to a gradual *reentry* into ministry, into my calling.

Waiting and the Discipline of Worship

The Acts of the Apostles reports that the disciples went to Jerusalem following the Ascension, where they waited for the fulfillment of the promise of the Holy Spirit, "constantly devoting themselves to prayer" (Acts 1:14a). God's spirit, from primal creation in Genesis, has always been involved in creation and in re-creation. The spirit, also translated "wind" or "breath," brings and maintains life. The Gospel of John talks about the need to be born of the spirit. This is God's work and nowhere is it more important than in the bringing to new life those of us who have been shattered by life-changing transitions, enormous loss, and deadening pain.

This work must be done by God's Spirit. We cannot do it. No one else can do it for us. We must not be indifferent, apathetic, or resistant to it. Instead, like the early disciples, we can give ourselves to the Spirit in the stillness of worship. Our task lies in devoting ourselves constantly to prayer. How easy it is to fall into self-pity, as Elijah did in his cave. How often we see others retreat into the darkness of themselves; the cave proves an apt image for anyone who trades creative waiting for isolation and self-pity.

A very powerful example of creative waiting comes to us from Mary, the mother of our Lord. Young, devout, innocent—she received the Annunciation in amazement. She had the spirit of devotion and trust, however, to be able to utter those most incredible words: "Here am I, the servant of the LORD; let it be with me according to your word" (Luke 1:38). Such trust derives only from worship.

Who were this girl's parents? What manner of home had been hers? How could someone, a girl in a male-dominated culture, learn the breadth and depth of Scripture found in the Magnificat? Where did she get her poetic gift? What was the source of her courage in facing a judgmental culture? If the disciples would much later be promised power after the Holy Spirit came upon them, Mary modeled that power more than thirty years earlier.

As an aside, I acknowledge that many scholars do not believe Mary spoke the Magnificat; in their judgment, it was composed by others and attributed to Mary. This had been done throughout Hebrew history, so it would have raised no eyebrows. I have chosen, however, to take the text at face value to illustrate a point. Now, back to Mary, pregnant with Jesus.

Hers would be nine months of waiting—waiting for the stirring inside her body to complement the stirring in her heart. Did Mary know Psalm 37?

> Wait for the LORD and keep to his way,
> and he will exalt you to inherit the land;
> you will look on the destruction of the wicked.
> (Psalm 37:34)

She waited, but not in silence. She composed and sang a hymn, the "Magnificat," from a whole collection of references in her Hebrew Bible; Psalm 37 sounds like a specific part of Mary's psalm.

The most powerful times of worship in my own period of gestation occurred at noon each Wednesday. I attended an Episcopal service of communion and healing. My fellow worshipers never numbered more than twenty; most had been attending this service regularly for several years. They welcomed me, heard my story, and shared their lives with me. Each Wednesday we went to the altar to receive communion and the laying on of hands for healing. My friend the priest, who had by then become my pastor, placed his hands upon our heads as we all held hands, and said, "(Wayne), because of your asking I affirm by faith that you have already been healed, and I anoint you with oil and lay my hands upon you in the name of the Father, and the Son, and the Holy Spirit."

Following this ritual, we gathered around a large table, ate lunch together, and studied Scripture. For some six months, I was privileged to meet with this group at God's altar. I came to a much fuller understanding of the difference between cure and healing. I have modified my pastor's words in my own ministry; I have chosen to say, "you are already *being* healed," because I realize that I may never be completely healed of what my life sustained. Even if such healing occurs, I will always need healing for other illnesses of body, mind, and spirit.

Bible stories and the psalms were also part of my daily waiting in worship. I gave more attention than at any other time in my life to the life of Jesus. What went on in his life during those years between ages twelve to thirty? Surely these were years of active waiting. How keenly aware he was of *kairos*—God's time—during his ministry. He talked often about his "hour," what God knew that no one else did. The forty days in the wilderness must have been a time of active waiting for God's word about Jesus' mission. His many times of withdrawing for solitary prayer were by definition times of worshipful waiting. Gethsemane must have been the most difficult, but again—worshipful waiting.

The prophet Isaiah offers a wonderfully poetic affirmation of waiting and worship.

> [T]hose who wait for the LORD shall renew their
>   strength,
> they shall mount up with wings like eagles,
> they shall run and not grow weary,
> they shall walk and not faint. (40:31)

The prophet admonishes his hearers with a promise; a psalmist gives testimony to personal experience of worshipful waiting.

> For God alone my soul waits in silence;
> from him comes my salvation.
> He alone is my rock and my salvation,
> my fortress; I shall never be shaken. (Psalm 62:1–2)

Many psalmists comment about personal experiences and admonitions to wait for God. "May integrity and uprightness preserve me, for I wait for you" (Psalm 25:21). "Be still before the LORD, and wait patiently for him" (Psalm 37:7). And who in the pain of loss and grief can fail to identify with the poet who says:

> I wait for the LORD, my soul waits,
> and in his word I hope;
> my soul waits for the LORD
> more than those who watch for the morning,
> more than those who watch for the morning.
> (Psalm 130:5–6)

Who in grief has no story to tell about long nights of sleeplessness? Reading fails to pass the time because powers of concentration have been dulled. The television carries station test patterns, info-mercials, boring repetitions of the daily news. Every sound by a passing automobile jerks us back into the present; the shadows that flicker in the windows remind us how slowly the clock moves. Yet nothing challenges our sadness like worshipful waiting—waiting for God and waiting with God. The waiting can include long nights of short prayers, one-sentence Scripture lessons, and an openness to the possibility that just because the voice of God is inaudible, it might still be heard.

Grief tends to exhaust us, while worship renews our energy. Whether our exhaustion is mental, emotional, or psychological, the breath, wind, or spirit of God gives new life. To wait before God reminds us of the enormity of the universe and of our solidarity with all who have ever grieved. To wait before God stirs within us the sense that we are not alone. To wait before God calls us beyond the suffering of the present and into hope for the future.

Worship provides solid and substantial content and context for healing. Obviously, the Bible, prayer, and corporate worship services offer excellent resources. The hymnals and recorded music help restore our lost songs. Two psalms in particular illustrate extremes of feeling, the depths of grief and the joy of deliverance: Psalm 137, written while the Jews were captive in Babylon, and Psalm 40, which reflects the psalmist's personal experience of being rescued from pain by God.

> On the willows there we hung up our harps.
> For there our captors asked us for songs,
> and our tormentors asked for mirth, saying,
> "Sing us one of the songs of Zion."
> How could we sing the LORD'S song in a foreign land?
> (Psalm 137:2–4 NRS)

> He put a new song in my mouth,
> a song of praise to our God. (Psalm 40:3)

Among the almost innumerable written resources for healing, I have found great strength in the *Book of Common Prayer* of the Episcopal Church. The Daily Office provides a systematic reading of the Bible over a two-year period and a reading of the psalms in a much shorter time frame. The offices for morning, noon, evening, and Compline provide succinct and uplifting lessons, songs, and prayers. They can be used in large gatherings, small groups, families, or by a single person.

Whatever context of worship one chooses, God can become our health and our salvation. God can give us back our music, even give us a new song.

Waiting and the Gift of Community

The pain of transition tends to impose a sense of isolation on us, even when we are around people. We feel like no one knows what we are experiencing or how we feel. In one sense, no one knows exactly how or what another person feels. Nevertheless, almost everyone knows something about pain, suffering, loss, and grief. From childhood onwards, we have learned what it feels like to hurt, to have lost something or someone important to us. Simply because no one else has ever had exactly the same experience as ours does not mean they know nothing of our sorrows. In fact, others who have been in the "miry bog" can sometimes serve as our guides through it and eventually out of it.

Psalm 27 has comforted and provided hope to countless people. The psalm begins with the affirmation that "The LORD is my light and my salvation; whom shall I fear?" Following a recitation of horrible circumstances, the poet concludes by speaking not only to himself, but to us as well: "Wait for the LORD; be strong, and let your heart take courage; wait for the LORD." Where do we find courage to wait creatively, especially when we have sunk so deep into pain? Certainly, the psalmist sets the context in worship—waiting for God. I would add that we also wait in community, and this sometimes requires both energy and courage. The times in which we feel the least like being with others may be the situations in which we most need others to support us, comfort us, and hold us accountable.

Suffering tends to isolate us, especially when we have difficulty admitting or accepting our vulnerability. The most difficult step for those suffering with an addiction, for example, is admitting the dependency. The same can be said about forgiveness: admitting we have sinned is the difficult first step to reconciliation. This is equally true of our suffering from loss, failure, and grief; we can admit we need God, our friends, and helping professionals.

At the deepest point of my own despair, four kinds of community assisted in my healing; three came to me unsolicited and the fourth accepted me when I turned to them. The first expression came from two close friends who intervened. They took an enormous risk. I could have rejected their admonition and withdrawn from them as friends. I could have lashed out at them in anger, told them to mind their own business; many people in pain do so. These two men, however, took a chance and said very clearly, "We are your friends; we cannot be your therapists. You must see a counselor and you must get on medication." The implication was almost tantamount to saying, "If you fail to do so on

your own, we will take you to the doctor ourselves."
They could see that I was not functioning well and
showed no indications of improvement. Because of their
concern, I called another friend who, several months
before, had offered to help me see his physician, a
prominent psychiatrist. I began soon after to take medication for anxiety and depression.

One of the primary roles our communities of healing
can play is that of evaluator. In the midst of suffering or
the dullness of depression, we ourselves cannot see much
of anything, much less our own condition. If ever we
need people to tell us the truth, hold us accountable,
push us toward change, it is in those times when grief
clouds our judgment and tears fog up the pathways.
Those fortunate enough to have loving and courageous
friends are blessed beyond words. Those of us who have
sufficient courage to trust such friends find that the difficult pathway to wholeness will be much less difficult
and not nearly so lonely as it might be without them.

The second part of my community structure has
been my family. At first I did not recognize them as a
part of my healing community; I saw them as simply
standing by. Until I began a program of therapy, including medication, I could not even understand their
involvement and the gift of their presence. In time I realized that my wife, daughters, sons-in-law, and brother
kept in constant contact with me throughout my ordeal.
The gift of their presence far outweighed any advice or
verbal encouragement they might have offered. The
seventeenth-century poet of *Paradise Lost*, John Milton,

suggested, "They also serve who only stand and wait." Such was the initial service of my family.

The philosopher of Ecclesiastes observed that there is "a time to keep silence, and a time to speak." My family understood the fine and often blurred line between those two times. I recall no time in which I wished they would do other than what they did. Their gift required sacrifice and courage, wisdom and perseverance.

The third component of my support system flowed in and out of my home like a gentle breeze. In addition to my two close friends, a large number of others presented themselves over a period of twelve to fifteen months. I had more friends than I realized. Letters and cards came from many parts of the country; during one extended period, I received an average of one flower arrangement a week. And always visits, some short and some longer.

The fourth component of my healing process proved to be the church, in retrospect not surprising. I now realize, however, the risk I took. After all, my church had inflicted the pain. I could easily have rejected the church in my disillusionment. Still, I turned again, as I had always done since childhood, to the church, knowing it to be an imperfect institution and a human organism. The church to which I turned was Episcopalian in its larger identity, but I had known the community of the specific parish for almost two decades. The priest was a longtime friend. In addition to the Wednesday noon Eucharistic and healing service mentioned earlier, I began to attend Sunday services. Although many members of the parish knew me as a prominent clergyman in the community, they allowed me to be no more than a communicant.

After attending the Eucharist and healing group for several months, I realized that healing was indeed taking place. I was eventually able to get through communion without heavy tears; I could talk about my pain without choking up. I began to share in the laughter and the teasing so valuable to groups who share their grief. I also began to experience—on a deeper level than I had ever known—the difference between a cure and healing. A cure would have meant the total elimination of the disease and perhaps all signs that it had ever been present. Healing meant that the pain, memory, scars, and emptiness would never be completely gone, but I would be able to embrace them and build on them. I have not experienced a cure, if by that term we mean the absence of all evidence of illness. However, I am experiencing healing and progress toward wholeness.

The sisters and brothers of this church became fellow sufferers and fellow singers in a chorus that knew both the sad songs and the happy ones. I stayed with them for six months, right in the seams between my period of letting go and my time of waiting. Waiting was less painful because the silence and the uncertainty were experienced jointly.

Many people who suffer at the hands of one community have every reason to be suspicious of all other communities and groups. When some speak glowingly of "family," the person who has been neglected or abused within or by a family may not feel warmth and gladness when that social unit is discussed. For a child who spent years in ridicule or alienation in school, the very thought of that social institution may call up negative emotions or even physical reactions. When a local church has inflicted pain upon an individual, the so-called Body of Christ may be perceived as the embodiment of evil.

Communities that fail us and that hold little likelihood for repentance and redemption must be rejected; appropriate substitutes are available. One's family of origin may have been severely dysfunctional, abusive, or criminal; surrogate families, however, can be discovered or created. Educational communities, workplaces, or social groups may also damage individuals, but other such communities that engender positive effects can be found. Certainly the same can be said for local churches. Perhaps the irony of such exchanges lies in the fact that we face the difficult task of letting go of the very community that has for so long been integral to what and who we are, and we wait in the company of another such faith community for whatever newness approaches us.

Whatever community we find, create, or discover in the "waiting place" serves several vital functions. The primary function of the community is to bear witness to hope, "the thing with feathers perches in the soul." As dark as our most intense grief may be, we find hope in the words, touches, prayers, and smiles of others. The very essence of community is communion, which means "at one with."

While the community offers hope, it also demands accountability. When the people who hold us in their arms and hearts see us using our grief irresponsibly, perhaps avoiding life and our work, they may well intervene. Their task requires discernment, wisdom, and courage. Black clothing may not be worn forever. The doors may not be closed and the shades drawn forever. Life goes on. The time limit for each person's grief varies, but our most intimate and trusted friends can tell us the truth and call us to account for our inaction, despair, and bitterness.

Our support communities also provide us with an environment in which to worship God. The Pentecost imagery is ideal for those who grieve, who doubt, whose futures are uncertain. The disciples lived through seven weeks of seeing Jesus and then not seeing him, grieving his death, and speculating about his absence. Their future hung in some unknown balance. The constant factor through days of uncertainty was their together- ness. Following the Ascension, their suspended time was given to prayer—probably in the Temple at the appointed hours—and together in that upper room.

Pentecost has always suggested mystery, creativity, and newness. The same Spirit that moved over the face of the deep in primal creation settled upon this little band of disciples centuries later. They were made new, but the manner of it remains a mystery. And so with those who navigate the waters of transition and suffer great losses. In the company of the church, even for those two or three gathered in his name, waiting becomes an exercise of faith grounded in hope.

The worshiping community is a place where the wonderful promise from Paul comes true: "No testing has overtaken you that is not common to everyone. God is faithful, and he will not let you be tested beyond your strength, but with the testing he will also provide the way out that you may be able to endure it" (1 Corinthians 10:13).

Other gifts of the worshiping community include laughter, singing, and rejoicing. We have already noted the place of worship and singing in our private devotional exercises. Perhaps in the early stages of our loss, and in our greatest pain, much of our worship will be private, or at least with a few select friends. As we begin to move outward, worship and rejoicing include more people and become less self-conscious.

I sat one day with a man who had been struggling with the consequences of a major health problem. He had been forced to adjust to a physical handicap. For many months, his emotional state seemed as precarious as his body. On the particular day we visited, I told him about a humorous situation in which I had been involved. He responded with a burst of spontaneous laughter that surprised him. He said to me, "That's the first time I remember laughing in more than a year." Just as community provides a safe place to cry, so it offers a setting for the healing power of laughter.

One of the most common reactions to great change and loss in our lives is to isolate ourselves; nearly everyone is tempted to do so. The surest pathway to healing and wholeness is populated with the worshiping community— many of whom have been where we are at one time or another—people who know the way back.

CHAPTER THREE

Transition and Healing: Testing the Waters

The process of letting go of our grief and what we have lost may require months and even years. For some, the timeline proves to be much shorter. No set rule exists. Nevertheless, time and healing smooth our jagged edges, our calendars begin to fill, our circle of friends and acquaintances expands. The winds subside and the seas calm down. If loss and grief tend to isolate us, active waiting tends to rebuild trust in the goodness of life; it does so through the people we allow to be close to us.

Part of the re-expansion of our lives involves facing the future without whatever and whomever we have left behind or lost completely. The future will bring more pain. The woman who has suffered a miscarriage or discovers that she will never bear a child must live in a world where babies seem to be everywhere. The person who has undergone a divorce often feels out of place at social functions, suspicious of the opposite sex, and even angry when observing couples holding hands or laughing. Even more difficult for a divorced person, the former spouse may still be a part of the lives of children, extended family, business concerns, or social structures.

Friendships often change after a great loss. The spouse dies and the survivor seems no longer able to fit into the dinner group or the bridge club. A child dies and the family friends with their children seem distant. Even the loss of a job may change one's social circle.

Many such changes involve secondary pain; that is, pain not nearly as severe as the primary loss, but still intense.

If we are to move beyond the most intense suffering, risk and courage will usher us into and ultimately through that grief of a secondary nature. The old adage, "The best way out is through," certainly holds true in dealing with the pain of any transition. Testing the waters of life in our new circumstances, although risky, sometimes brings pleasant surprises, even occasional serendipity. One primary indicator of a successful reentry into our routines—and even the exploration of completely new ones—is humor. A family with whom I have been very close for many years lost a young man in the prime of life. On holidays in particular, when the family gathers, his absence is especially conspicuous. But they always include him. We call the remembering part of those gatherings the "Pete stories." Many of the stories are bittersweet and some are refreshingly funny; they keep alive Pete's memory while providing ongoing healing for the family.

Moving out of isolation also involves seeing humor in our situation, taking ourselves less seriously, allowing the attention of others to go elsewhere instead of remaining fixed upon our grieving self. When we can laugh at ourselves and permit others to direct humor our way, the horizon expands, the world proves to be larger, and we have more room in which to explore, move, and grow. Such humor, willingness to be surprised, and lightness of spirit also allow others to relax around us. I visited a woman who had undergone several serious illnesses and surgeries. I asked her several questions about her struggles with ill health and she answered them without a trace of self-pity. Finally, she grinned and said, "Now that's enough about me; let's talk about other things." I had no sense that she was denying her condition. She was simply moving away from the self-absorption that such illnesses inflict upon us, at least for a time.

Those who attempt to be present with the bereaved find that prolonged intensity makes relationships difficult. What does one say after months of the same discussion? How much silent sitting and waiting is helpful? How many times must a dear friend hear the same stories before grief becomes self-pity and close friends fill the role of validator? And with new friends, how much and how soon do we share our loss and pain? Moving from the isolation of letting go and into the task of active waiting requires some testing of the waters—temperature, depth, tides, and cleanness. The waters are always more easily tested when they calm down. The tester must be resolute, steady, and careful. Above all, such active waiting means listening, watching, and expecting. Of course life will never be the same, but whatever life brings or whatever we create can be surprising and joyful. After my own most recent loss, I began to test the Episcopalian waters—so different from my Baptist background and yet not unfamiliar to me. While proceeding toward Episcopal ordination to Holy Orders, I was asked by several diocesan officers, "What are your goals and expectations two, three, four years from now?" I had no answer to that question at the beginning. I had lived my life by schedules, timetables, and goals. My great loss opened a new door; for the first time in my life I was free—and willing—to be surprised.

Others commented about the courage I must have had to take such a step—especially "at your age." I suppose courage was required; certainly every step along the way included risk. But I found myself regaining my sense of humor little by little, becoming less self-centered, and feeling more relaxed. In fact, many of my friends affirmed and validated my new direction and buoyed my confidence.

Three days after my week of ordination examinations, I was called, interviewed, and ultimately employed as an assistant minister in a church not far from my home. The months that followed have been one surprise after another. I have been learning to trust a congregation again, to offer my ministry, and to reveal more and more about who I am. I fully expect these pleasant surprises to continue.

Moving out of isolation and into a mode of active waiting carries at least one powerful dis-ease—a kind of paranoia, suspicion, over-carefulness. Having been burned by a hot stove, we tend to be more careful around all stoves. A parent who has lost a child tends to be overly cautious with any other children in the family. A person who has been divorced may be distrustful of all persons of the opposite sex. One who has suffered severe disappointment in a physician, a member of the clergy, a church, or a close friend may view all other such persons and institutions with caution or even distrust. A certain amount of anxiety may not be bad, however, if it causes us to be a bit more careful of boundaries. Too much suspicion can and probably will make testing the waters difficult and make diving in impossible. Risk and courage, however, offer great rewards—in spite of the discomfort of painful memories and the possibility of new losses. One of those rewards may be the ability to affirm the full humanity of oneself and others, as well as the essential goodness of life. Death is in fact a part of life. Furthermore, the rhythms of life are seldom "fair." Babies die. Good people contract horrible diseases. Major conflicts occur in almost every life at one time or another. Workers are not always treated properly. Relationships end in death, divorce, or breaches of understanding. Somewhere in the relative distance, however, healing reaches the point of endurable scars, people are seen as flawed but essentially good, life as precious and worth celebrating.

Three issues already alluded to affect the timing and the process of testing the waters: trust, risk, and courage. A bit more needs to be said about each.

Trust, when broken, requires more time and effort to heal and be restored than any other loss. Perhaps it is not too much to say that almost every great loss involves broken trust of something or someone—God, friends, health, relationships, and even life itself. Elderly people who begin to lose physical capacities suffer falls, drop or spill things, and may lose confidence in their own bodies. The person who has broken a hip may fear going out of the house because of the possibility of another fall. The betrayal of a friendship often causes the person wronged to keep others at arm's length. Small children whose parents divorce may distrust adults who wish to provide them with stable and secure environments. Personal failure may result in difficulty trusting one's self, one's judgment, and even one's own ability. Whatever has inflicted loss and pain affects trust.

Whether or not we fully understand what is happening to us and find words to verbalize distrust, we face a clear choice. We can remain in the relative isolation of our early and most intense grief, or we can begin to move outward in an effort to rebuild and relearn trust. Of course, the choice will not always settle at one extreme or the other; most of us drift back and forth and eventually settle somewhere between the extremes. Trust often returns gradually, as we find others to be worthy of trust, as we succeed in new efforts and relationships, and as we begin to heal from our most bitter pain. That process will be more likely and will occur more quickly if we are conscious of both our distrust and of our need to move forward.

To trust again, we need to assess our expectations. Every human being we know and love will disappoint us somewhere along the line. Every career, every neighborhood, every institution will disappoint us at times. Trust sometimes suffers the most severe damage when we expect more of people and institutions than they can possibly deliver.

Being aware of our unreasonable expectations can help us to act cautiously as we *risk* putting our feet into the water. Wes was a forty-six-year-old widower of eighteen months. He had two children in college and a demanding job. He dealt with his grief by becoming more deeply invested in his work and in his son and daughter. He could not compensate for his loneliness, however. His minister confronted him with the question: "What are you doing about your loneliness?" Wes had not admitted to being lonely, but the pastor's question named the demon. Wes admitted that his loneliness was made worse because he feared intimacy, remarriage, and the possibility of another loss. He was afraid to even ask someone out to dinner. Wes was clearly stuck.

Ella serves as another example. She had been a successful office administrator for several years. Her family moved to another community, so she sought and found a similar job there. After a few months, she realized the new office was in turmoil and she resigned. She found another job quickly, but a controlling and harassing supervisor dominated the new workplace. When she talked with him about how she felt, he fired her. She later said that she was embarrassed, had lost confidence in herself, and for a time became a homemaker to avoid other people and another workplace.

Trust proved difficult for both Wes and Ella to regain. One's future always depends upon developing healthy and mature trust in others and in life itself. Trust also involves a careful look at our expectations.

Indeed, getting on with one's life following a great loss takes time and more than trust and risk. At some point, it also takes *courage*. One of the most unforgettable people I ever met was a woman in her sixties who lost her husband to cancer. He had taken care of their finances, transportation, and all business matters. She seemed as lost as anybody I ever knew. But within months she went to driving school, bought an automobile, found a job, and began to blossom. She dealt with her grief beautifully because somewhere deep inside herself, with help from her friends, she found the courage to take some chances on her future. Part of her courage came from her willingness to trust an uncertain future.

Trust, courage, and risk help us to accept the often disorderly process of letting go, waiting, and moving forward.

Although I have discussed letting go, waiting, and reaching out in an orderly sequence, the process is seldom so neat. Many who suffer losses and grief find themselves doing all three all along the way. The very act of letting go of anger, resentment, guilt, shame, embarrassment, and what or whom we have left behind includes reaching out to whatever can fill the empty places in our lives. These early explorations, however, tend to be tenuous and sporadic at best. Therefore, we need creative and active waiting and a large helping of patience. In the silence of life's major changes, losses, and emptiness, we have the opportunity to watch and listen to ourselves and to everything around us. During and following our acts of release and our time of waiting, we assess the areas and experiences that can draw us forward. We test them, pass through them, consider them, and make them a serious matter for prayer. If we find sufficient value in these low-risk efforts, we move another step in the same direction. If not, we pause, wait, and consider another direction. So much of our recovery from grief involves trial and error. We tend to move three steps forward and two steps back. Over a longer period, however, we make significant process.

My own unscientific observations tell me that most people do in fact move beyond intense grief and into some measure of health and wholeness on the other side of their transitions. People refer to the great "hole" in their lives, the "terrible scar," the "hollow place," the "crack" that runs through the self. People say they have been changed by their experiences. All the images are apt and valid. Yet, most of these people have also learned to let go of what they have lost, even while they retain powerful memories. They invest themselves in some form of creative waiting while they recover. They test the waters of new streams and oceans and eventually learn to swim in the deep places. They again come to trust their environments and their own resilience. Some cautions are in order, however.

The Process of Moving Forward

Early in the loss and grief experience, friends and professionals make themselves available to us. But as days turn into weeks and weeks into months, many of these people become less present and available. After all, they have many other demands upon them. Somewhere in our journey, as our helping persons are less involved, and

out of the most desperate places of our sorrow, we realize we need more specific and structured help. One such
resource may be a support group. Carefully defined support groups can provide the direction, checks and bal-
ances, and accountability that our family and closest
friends cannot.

Many such groups have been formed through local
churches and hospitals. One of these is called Compassionate
Friends; it has provided support for thousands of people
whose children have died. But three or more such people in the same church or community can easily form a
group of their own, with minimal help from a minister
or professional counselor.

In addition to but not in lieu of such groups, psycho-
therapists who specialize in grief work and the work of
helping people through transitions sometimes prove to
be invaluable. The professionals are not our friends or
family members; therefore, they are able to be more
objective. Their most helpful functions may be to assess
our progress, to identify indicators that our grief is making us physically or mentally ill, and to suggest methods
to help us get unstuck.

Educational materials and the stories of others provide an additional set of helps. Many of them provide
some good basic information as well as starter themes
that enable group members to talk about their experiences, feelings, and progress. When we begin to listen to
our own feelings, counselors and fellow group members
are able to respond and hold us accountable when we
lapse into self-pity, isolation, and bitterness; they can

also affirm those feelings that are normal and that contribute to our progress. Together, the educational materials and our support system help us with both the letting go tasks and the waiting process; they also encourage us to explore the next steps we must take to move forward with our lives.

I think about Winnie the Pooh who visited Rabbit and ate too much honey. He got so big he couldn't squeeze out of the hole in which Rabbit lived. In his stuck position, his friends waited with him and sang comforting songs until he "went down." Our best friends are those who provide a safe and positive place in which to wait, but who also confront us when we are unwilling to do the hard work of letting go, waiting, and testing the waters.

Friends, support groups, and professionals also help us measure the pace of our journey. If we become overly impatient, they remind us that time is a healing agent and that it needs to be respected. In a dark moment in my own life, a friend reminded me that time was then very much on my side, that I could not and should not move too quickly out of the pain nor allow myself to become stuck in it. Friends help us to avoid becoming myopic; they also help us to avoid channels too deep and currents too swift to manage. Those who emerge from great losses and deep pain also emerge from some social and functional isolation. Recreating our lives after a loss requires the wisdom and support of others; those who serve us best love us deeply but manage to maintain some objectivity.

Let me offer one last observation about grief and suffering: look for serendipity, surprise, beauty, color, laughter, and celebration. As we begin to emerge from our deepest grief and test the future, every success encourages additional effort and risk. Every compliment from others builds renewed self-confidence. Every smile from another person enables us to smile in return. Any conversation with another person in which we are able to listen rather than talk, to concentrate on that person rather than on our own pain, and to offer some encouragement is a step in the right direction.

CHAPTER FOUR

Resurrection

There are some defeats more triumphant than victories!

Christians are people of the cross and people of the resurrection. Prosperity tends to dull our awareness of the passion of Jesus; adversity forces us back to what and who we really are because of the cross. The Episcopal "Blessing of a Marriage" begins with this sentence: "Most gracious God, we give you thanks for your tender love in sending Jesus Christ to come among us, to be born of a human mother, and to make the way of the cross to be the way of life." The way of the cross to be the way of life. Everything about human nature and our culture shuns such a position. Even in the first century, Paul acknowledged that his culture looked upon the cross as a scandal. So, what makes the way of the cross the way of life?

The way of the cross forces us to recognize that only through suffering does the redemption process make any sense. Jesus suffered for us and was glorified, "by his bruises we are healed" (Isaiah 53:6). In our baptism we identify with his suffering so that we might be raised to walk in the newness of life (Romans 6). Suffering comes as an inevitable part of life, sometimes as an accident of the willy-nilly nature of the universe, sometimes because of our poor decisions and choices, and sometimes as a result of the presence of evil. Whatever its source, suffering is part of the human condition and nearly always involves loss and grief. The question is never, "Will I suffer?" but "When and how will I suffer?" Neither should we expect that having sustained one such blow, we earn the right to be free of pain for the rest of our lives.

Redemptive suffering is part of the Christian life. It is the way of life for those who follow Jesus, a way of life that leads somewhere. I have discovered that my own life changes, failures, losses, grief, and pain have shaped who and what I am as a person and as a follower of Jesus Christ. I was unable to understand this during my darkest times. I could not hear the truth or accept it, no matter who told me or how graciously they tried to explain it. I would not have believed it to be true even if I had received the message from an angel. Only in retrospect do we begin to realize that out of our own losses has come a gentler, humbler, and more empathetic soul. Only in hindsight do we come to accept and embrace our own vulnerability. Only in our vulnerability do we achieve true intimacy with ourselves and with other people. This is part of the way of the cross and the resurrection.

The way of the resurrection leads to new life. We tend to miss resurrection in the here and now and focus only on new life. Yet Jesus was resurrected in this life and only later ascended into that life to come. I often wonder if the life of the resurrection begins when we learn to live the way of the cross. After all, what need would we have for resurrection apart from death? We face many lesser deaths in our losses here on earth.

Think about those many deaths. The sleep in the night suggests the death of the day past. We lose our pets, our innocence, our childhoods, some friends along the way, some physical skills, children who move away, sometimes our marriages, and almost always our health. We lose positions we once held, sometimes titles and influence. We may lose wealth. The list is endless. Yet, in these deaths, the people of God find new life in the life of the resurrection. Out of every loss can come new life.

The process involves three stages: separation, crossing some chasm, and incorporation into something new, or letting go, waiting, reentry or transformation or resurrection. The loss involves some kind of death, good-bye, departure, pain, sorrow, darkness, grave-like hopelessness. The greater the loss, the more intense the depth of pain and the sense of death. The Christian affirmation, however, points us from life as it has been, through whatever we can describe as a kind of death, to some kind of new life. I contend that the resurrection is at work in the here and now; it can be a part of every change in our lives. The new life on the other side of the chasm becomes the transformed life, renewed and even remade, able to touch the lives of others out of our loss, vulnerability, and transformation.

Jane Hamilton, a contemporary novelist, begins her novel *A Map of the World* with these words: "I used to think if you fell from grace it was more likely than not the result of one stupendous error, or else an unfortunate accident. I hadn't learned that it can happen so gradually you don't lose your stomach or hurt yourself in the landing. You don't necessarily sense the motion" (New York: Bantam Doubleday, 1999). Well into my twenties, I thought that loss of innocence, the fracturing of overwrought idealism, or awakening from an adolescent sense of being entitled to a pain-free life, would come about in one cataclysmic event. Now, after three such events and many smaller ones, I am convinced that I am still losing my innocence, refining my idealism into something more akin to spiritual vision, and recognizing that loss, pain, and grief keep coming for all of us. Until my own most recent transition, I had not been able to embrace the pain and use it as a window into my own soul. Bruises and scars have little value as badges of honor; their real worth lies in pointing us toward resurrection and new life in the One whose suffering redeemed the world.

Everybody experiences transitions almost continually. Babies are born, grow up, leave home as adults, go to college or work, retire, age, die. We all experience bouts of ill health, make friends, lose friends. We change in good ways and in difficult ways. The major differences in our life changes seem to be of kind and degree. Each of us can look back on our own lives and try to think of a time when nothing was changing; we probably will not remember any such time. The difficult transitions are those that require the most help; they are also those that promise the greatest possibilities for growth.

Clergy enjoy a privilege open to no other professional: the privilege of entering the homes and families of parishioners during their very intimate experiences.

When a loved one dies, the funeral professionals and friends and neighbors come and go; the clergy are invited to come, stay a while, and share in the deepest memories of those who grieve. The clergy have a unique role when a baby is born, a marriage is celebrated, and a major anniversary is observed. The parish priest hears the stories, waits amidst the brokenness, and shares the tears when a marriage collapses. Ministers hear the most private and personal stories, stories that may never have been told aloud. I try never to take that privilege lightly.

My own experience with people in transition constantly inspires me. The courage and resilience of the human spirit remind me that we are all made in the image and likeness of God; surely God provides us with the strength to endure and to rise above the difficult changes life sends our way. Survival, however, can happen without really advancing our lives. The people I most admire are those who have survived difficult transitions and gone beyond what they were before the crisis.

Saint Paul recites a list of adversities (Romans 8:35–36) and then affirms that "we are more than conquerors through him who loves us" (Romans 8:37 NRSN). Those who navigate life's changes most successfully finally come to a better place or condition than they had ever experienced. And heaven watches, even as it helps. We can look again to a text from Saint Paul cited earlier: "In my opinion whatever we may have to go through now is less than nothing compared with the magnificent future God has planned for us. The whole creation is on tiptoe to see the wonderful sight of the sons [and daughters] of God coming into their own (Romans 8:18–19, translation by J. B. Phillips).

Bryant Kirkland, longtime beloved minister of the Fifth Avenue Presbyterian Church in New York City, often told newcomers, "You can't go it alone in New York." We cannot go through difficult transitions alone, either. Nor must we. God has promised the Holy Spirit to comfort and direct us. God has given us Holy Scripture to teach and inspire us. God has given us the church to help us and heal us. God has given us trustworthy professionals, groups of friends, and gracious loved ones to sit with us, journey with us, and ultimately to celebrate with us.

At the end of his life and just before the children of Israel were to go into the Promised Land, Moses gave a long speech. In one admonition, he envisioned the day when the wandering would end. He told the Israelites to take baskets of the fruit of the land, set them before the priests and the Levites, affirm their faith, and remember their journey. Then they were to use that very produce to celebrate, to throw a big party, if you will (Deuteronomy 26:1–11).

One day we will smile and laugh and sing and play again. One day we will remember the good things before the transition began. One day we will create more good things, even as God creates us into new people of God.